EXTRA POINTS

The Life of My Story

Coach Keith Howard

Foreword by Howard J. Clay Jr.

Extra Points is the unforgettable, motivating journey of Coach Howard, a man who understands life and what it means to overcome life's obstacles. Coach Howard presents his story in a journey that will take you through the wins and losses of his extraordinary, unpredictable life from the time he was a young teenager, till today.

Let's face it, growing up in today's world is challenging, but growing up as a minority with big dreams is filled with even more adversities. Coach Howard's Book, <u>Extra Points: The Life of My Story</u> takes us deep into the events of Coach Howard's life to witness how he handled some of the issues facing young, black men today. From racism during his early days at University of Pittsburgh to losing a $15 million fortune, we follow him through life's ups and downs. We read about his struggles with loved ones and his battles with depression. In the end, we learn how he handled each roller coaster in his life and how it all made him the successful man he is today.

Along with telling his life's story, Coach Howard also aims to motivate young men to keep moving forward and stay positive with some practical advice he calls, "Extra Points." These "Extra Points" are included to provide the reader an extra boost of motivation to reach success. Coach Howard's goal for "Extra Points" is to reach young men where they are in life and encourage them to get to where they want to be.

www.extrapointsllc.com

Tracy,
Our friendship is so
very timeless. Please
continue to prosperous.
I'm proud of you.

Keith Howard.

Chapters

Dedication

... to each and every player who has ever prepared, practiced and participated in a game I have coached.

EXTRA
POINTS
The Life of My Story

Coach Keith Howard

Foreword by
Howard J. Clay Jr.

About 3 years ago, I had the pleasure of speaking at a convention in Washington DC. It was exciting because I'd never been to DC or the DC area. I was one of four speakers that was to speak about entrepreneurship and leadership to a room of over 300 young men. When I arrived, my friend took me straight to the convention. I looked over the program, and saw the other speakers. I had never heard of any of them as I'm sure they had never heard of me. But one name caught my eye- Keith Howard. I remember leaning over to my friend and saying jokingly, "His name is Howard, so he better be good!" Coach Howard was scheduled to go up right before me. I sat up in my chair, in anticipation and I wasn't disappointed. Coach Howard was amazing! The crowd was energetic and enthusiastic after he was finished which in turn, made it easier for me and my speech. After I finished speaking, I said to myself, "I have to meet this guy." I walked over to him, introduced myself and we began to talk. It was an instant synergy! It felt like I grew up with this guy. We decided to go to lunch after the program and we've been friends ever since. The thing that impressed me the most was how genuine and honest he was. He was very transparent and that was refreshing. He wasn't full of himself and he was able to proudly say when he was wrong or made a mistake, and you don't find too many men like that. During our conversation he told me he was finishing up his book called Extra Points: The Life of my Story." I replied, "Can't wait!"

Many of the minority young men today unfortunately still have an uphill climb to success, with no guidance. Through all of my mentoring programs and schools, I still see a lot of young men who go in the wrong directions and make bad decisions. Decisions that I feel could be avoided, if they were shown the right way. This is more prevalent in sports. Many of the athletes are just judged by their talents and are given special treatment, instead of corrective direction. That is why I'm excited about

Coach Howard's Book, Extra Points. It deals with these issues head on and gives real life situations as examples of hardships and struggles. But the greatest thing it gives is a "solution". Actual "Extra Points" are added to each chapter to make sure the main points are brought into focus, for the young men to understand.

Over many years, Coach Howard has coached and mentored thousands of young men, of all races, and helped them achieve better lives and careers. He took his own mentorship that he received from great coaches and men and passed it on to the youth and to the readers. We get to see a rare glimpse of what it takes to be successful after catastrophic failures and disappointment. Coach Howard is not afraid to go there, as long as the reader can learn from it. These examples and stories are priceless, especially for the youth at those critical decision making years.

Many of young men he has mentored have gone on to do great things. Whether on or off the field, in the streets, or in the classroom, Coach Howard's passion is to change lives for the better. Through this book, he wants to accomplish the same thing.

This book is an easy read for any young adult that may be dealing with any hardships or lacking sense of direction. This book is full of jewels and testimonies that will encourage, uplift, and help move you forward. Any man that losses 15 Million dollars and still is successful, is worth reading about. His story is unique and is universal to the plythe of a young black man.

Without question I recommend this book to everyone and anyone that has a dream, that wants to be better, and that wants to move in the right direction in their lives. Hardships will come, hard times will come, but with the help of a few "Extra Points" you will make it through.

Congratulations to Coach Howard as he takes his passion to the next level and becomes a Published Author! Many lives will be changed, many young men will find the direction and help they need.

Testimonials

Keith Howard's life work is dedicated to mentoring and developing young males. He has a passion to help these boys grow into the respectable young men that they are destined to become. Whether on the football field or through mentoring organizations like Team Focus, Coach Howard has impacted the lives of countless boys and young men across the country.

Mike Gottfried
Former NCAA Head Football Coach and
ESPN College Football Analyst
Founder of "Team Focus"

I have known Coach Howard for over 20 years! Coach was a part of our staff, when I played football as a student-athlete at the University of Pittsburgh. Keith and I developed a great relationship and he always demonstrated a passion to help people! Keith's new book is a powerful testimony of overcoming and never quitting! I would encourage the student-athlete, coach, business owner, or teacher to read Keith's new book! It will be life changing for you!

Todd Pipkin,
Head of School
Rocky Mount Prep

"Father, Mentor, Coach, Radio Personality" we now can add "Author" to the list and the depth of Coach Howard.
Coach is a man that wants to improve his community. He is not just a hearer of the community issues and problems but a doer. Someone that makes an impact with all that he does and everyone he meets!!

Coach Bryce K. Bevill
Director of Player Development
University of Maryland Football Team

In my role as President/CEO at Bishop McNamara High School, I have had the good pleasure to interact with and observe Keith Howard for nearly 20 years—as a coach, colleague, business owner, and most importantly, as a father. The first words that come to mind when describing him are class and character. He is a man of integrity and a great role model for us all.

Dr. Marco J. Clark '85
President/CEO
Bishop McNamara High School

Wisdom comes from experience, and Coach Howard is an example of just that. I've had the pleasure to both play for and coach with Coach Howard at different levels of football, and the most important thing I took away from those experiences is how much I learned from him. Coach Howard pushed everyone around him to be better and to grow, and I know that this book will do the same. Coach Howard taught hundreds of young men some of the most important values in becoming strong men. Through his life experiences – the ups and the downs – this book will help its readers put their lives into perspective, and will most importantly help them to learn and grow.

Miniard Culpepper Jr.
Former Football player for the Catholic University of America and played for Coach Howard

I am so very proud of you. You have come so far from our elementary school playground to the board room to the football field to the motivational speaker stage. It is wonderful to see you take all that you have learned on your own journey and share it with others so that their journey might be easier or more fulfilling. You have worked so hard and been a mentor to so many. Through this book, you now have an opportunity to reach so many more. I am certain that "Extra Points" will positively impact the lives of youth and adults alike. Continued blessing to you so that you may continue to bless others.

Kara Freeman Lee
IT Executive

Coach Howard provides unique insight that will help youth develop into future leaders on and off the field. Players and coaches will highly benefit from his teachings.

Dell Robinson
Life long College Athletics Administrator
Former Commissioner of the Great Lakes Intercollegiate Athletics Conference

"Keith Howard offers both the youthful and more seasoned reader a wellspring of inspiration fueled by lived experiences that encompasses both trials and triumphs as an entrepreneur, corporate executive, coach, son and father. Keith's transparency is a refreshing approach to the literary and rhetorical art of motivating others to dare to dream as well as to even embrace the journey of discovering countless life lessons learned through the "fumbles" and major losses in life that can potential serve as a vehicle toward greater success."

Gregory M Howard
Homiletics Instructor at the Samuel DeWitt Proctor School of Theology at Virginia Union University in Richmond VA and Senior Pastor of First Baptist Church East End in Newport News VA.

Coach Howard epitomizes hard work, discipline, excellence, and inner strength. He leads by example and has a long track record of helping young men reach their personal, athletic, and academic potential. More importantly Coach Howard is a man of character who looks to empower people so that they view obstacles in life as learning moments that shape you positively as a person. His wisdom and courage to confront mediocrity on the football field and in life had provided him a unique perspective on how to best motivate people, which is a rarity. Coach Howard, the world has been waiting for you!!!

Marcal Graham, Ed.D
University of Maryland Educational Opportunity Center 2016

I met Coach Howard in 2005 at the Team Focus Camp
for boys. He has been a mentor to my son for many years.
Coach Howard is a wonderful mentor who truly cares about
the young men and their futures. I remember the time
he drove three hours to Williamsburg, VA to meet several
young men. He talked to each of them and their moth-
ers then drove back to MD. He would even make a trip to
Hampton or Richmond VA, to attend basketball games of
not one but several of the boys all on the same day. He is a
dedicated coach and father who shows that same love and
care to those he mentors. Thank you Coach Howard for
taking the time to care and provide direction to my son who
is now a Senior at VCU.

Yvette Nazien
Mother of a child mentored by Coach Howard

Introduction

It's funny that the first speech I ever wrote inspired me to write this book. During that speech, entitled "DreamOn,"I taught audiences the seven characteristics I have used in my own life to win at "life." Throughout my coaching career, I have taken the best attributes of winning coaches that I have been around both on the field and off the field and created a seven characteristic play book for winning. As I track the life of my story, I want to recognize a few coaches who made a tremendous impact on me and helped me without even knowing it to develop DREAMON and eventually write this book.

DISCIPLINE was the first characteristic introduced to me and just about every coach I've had displayed different levels of discipline, but none more than my own parents and teachers in elementary school. Weldon and Rita Howard quite simply taught me right from wrong early in life and enforced consequences when I did wrong and recognized me when I did right. It sounds sort of simple but looking at the ills of our society today around customer service, soft skills and just overall being a good citizen, maybe it's not so simple after all. I can remember my parents and elementary teachers constantly setting discipline as a foundation for my life. Thanks, Mom and Dad...thanks to all my elementary teachers.

RESPECT would be the next characteristic. The coach who taught me the most about respect is a tough selection as so many have used this characteristic, however it probably was Coach Joe Gibbs, former Head Coach of the Washington Redskins. This example is interesting because I only met him once in passing, but I watched him from afar as a fan of the Washington Redskins. Coach Gibbs always talked about respecting yourself, respecting the game, respecting your teammates, opponents and officials. Even though he won three Super Bowls, he always took time to do it with the respect of the opponent. In a violent highly emotional game such as football, this sort of leadership is few and far between. Each week, Coach Gibbs would be respectful of his players, opponents and officials and I could see why he was winning in life. Thanks, Coach Gibbs, for teaching by example.

EDUCATION was the next characteristic. Initially, while in elementary and secondary school, I was under the impression that the more textbook education you had, the better your quality of life. However, over a period of time, I learned that non-traditional education and experiences are just as valuable. While so many coaches have taught me the importance of education, overall, I would explore, discover and learn on my own, which was the best education I could have learned.

ACHIEVEMENT is the next characteristic. Yes... just winning...the coach who helped me with this is also my life's coach and football coach from the University of Pittsburgh, Mike Gottfried. I can't say enough about Coach Gottfried but I will say he taught me several things about achieving. First, he instilled a burning desire in me to win. That winning wasn't just for a game but for life: "Win in everything you do." I also learned the importance of helping others win, on and off the field. Coach Gottfried also taught me how much preparation and sacrifice is needed in order to win. I would watch him draw football plays on napkins during meals always attempting to get an edge on the opponent. This is a practice I still use today, both drawing plays on napkins and writing speeches on napkins. I watched him go without sleep for hours and hours on end yet was fresh as a daisy when, as he would say, the lights come on. Thanks, Coach Gottfried, for everything.

MOTIVATION was something that I learned was an important characteristic of winning. I also learned the fact that not everyone can motivate. It's an innate skill. It's God's gift. I can remember how many coaches/mentors motivated me. I can also remember being able to motivate myself and my teammates, friends, family, etc. From my first coach (Coach Mitch), till today I've observed coaches motivate in their own way. Even when I watch videos of NFL coaches jumping, yelling, doing whatever is necessary to motivate their professional teams. There is one though... one person who has continuously been a motivator to me... he isn't a coach, elected official or a business man; he's just a guy. His name is Kenny Jones. Kenny Jones is my cousin. Kenny and I have been joined at the hip since we were born. He is a year older than me but my biggest fan. No one has supported me and motivated me more than he can even know. The beauty of it is he does it the right way...with love. See, Kenny will be the first to tell you, "College wasn't for me." Kenny will be the first to tell you he wakes up every morning at 6am, starts his truck and drives his dump truck all day. But what's great about Kenny is he is just a humble guy who knows when to tell me the REAL truth. Nobody on this planet has been more of a motivator to me than Kenny. I just don't ever want to let the guy down. He never went to a public speaking class but he tells it like it is and it inspires me. That inspiration allows me to drive, push, and strain and keep pursuing my dreams and to help so many others pursue theirs. Thanks, Kenny Jones...just a regular guy motivating me to be an extraordinary guy.

I've learned this about making dreams come true. You must be *ORGANIZED*. When I say organized, I don't mean neat or orderly...I mean three things: You must know who you are; Where you are going; and how you are going to get there. There must be a plan. Everything I do is with a plan. A well thought-out, specific, measurable, achievable, realistic and time-sensitive plan. The person who helped me with this organization the most is a coach but also my very best friend, Tim Washington. "Wash", as I call him, has stood witness while watching and sharing my dreams come true. He has done it in a quiet way...by being organized. Wash and I met on the football field when we were ten years old and he's been making sure I stay organized ever since. While at PITT, Wash and I learned from the greatest coaches, managers, administrators, trainers, even the grounds crew took time to teach us. Wash would say to me all the time, "Man, we are made to coach." We are football coaches and we have a certain standard. We enhanced and honed that standard and even though were weren't the most successful in early years, Wash kept sticking to the plan and making sure I did. But here's the great thing about Wash, he never wanted any fanfare. He was humble. That was the secret sauce to our success. Yes, OUR success on the field as coaches and as best friends in life. Wash told everyone who he is…a great coach who was making sure our plan stayed in effect so we could get where we are going. Wash never wavered nor did he allow me to waver on how we were going to get there, which was staying true to the plan.

TEAMWORK is my final valuable characteristic of leadership. This selection was easy, it's Bernice Nickens. My grandmother was the kindest person I ever met! She had eleven children. She lived in a modest house and worked a modest job. She went to church every Sunday and made the best biscuits, sweet potato pie and pancakes ever. I can remember being five years old playing in her kitchen, while she prepared a meal with the help of large family. My grandmother had an uncanny knack of getting the team to work. Everyone put aside egos, agendas, etc. I used to wonder when I got older how someone so gentle and so kind got so many to work in the same direction for the same common good. It was when she passed away that I figured out how. She started and integrated the whole team and the team was the family. Grandma was all about the family. She had all the assets of a leader. Grandma was a real matriarch. Now, I look at my own daughters, Kennedy and Fallon and I see, 105 years later, the same kind, gentle leadership in them, that I saw in my grandmother. I love my grandmother and without a doubt she taught me the importance of teamwork and it begins with the family. Thanks, Grandma. I miss you.

This is me, Coach Howard. Now sit back as I take you through the Life of MY STORY! May you gain as much from reading it as I did writing it.

Chapter One

"Having a Dream"

April 4, 1968. For some people who read this, they know exactly where they were and what they were doing. The day is historic for a very tragic reason. On this day, Nobel Peace Prize winner and Civil Rights icon, Dr. Martin Luther King Jr. was assassinated. For me, I was celebrating my first full day on Earth. Well, I was born on April 3. Of course, I have no memory of what was going on, where I was or what was happening, but I understand the enormity of the moment.

Now, I do have the stories my mom used to share with me when I became older. Mom would tell me how Washington DC was ablaze. People were looting in the streets. It was chaos. I can remember my mom telling me how my dad had to venture out to Manassas, Virginia, just to retrieve some formula for me. If you know DC traffic, you know that was a long way, especially back in the late

60's.

While I surely don't believe there was any correlation between Dr. King's assassination and my birth (maybe a little), I started to really think about his death and my birth a few years ago. I can remember being in elementary school and there was a conversation around actually having a national holiday to recognize Dr. King's birthday. I remember sitting in my 6th grade class and thinking..."there's no way that will ever happen." I also would read what a great man Dr. King was and how his birthday should be recognized, but I still didn't believe it would happen.

Low and behold, it did. In 1983, President Ronald Reagan declared the third Monday in January as "Dr. Martin Luther King Jr. Day ". From that moment on, I really started to pay attention to the great Dr. King. I read. I watched movies. I wanted to get to know who this great man was, who was killed the day after I was born, that shocked the world.

Once I got older and started working, I used to take the holiday for granted. I would use it as a day of rest, like many other Americans do. However, it was a

Catholic University in 2007 that I changed how I spent King Day. At Catholic University, the football team was predominantly made up of white players and coaches. The head coach, Dave Dunn, decided that King Day was going to be a "day of service." I was surprised. Coach Dunn had the team visit an elementary school and we spent the day painting the school. The day of service, predominantly involving white players and coaches, is the moment I woke up.

Going forward, I decided that my King Days were going to be of service as well. The services I chose ranged from working at a soup kitchen, taking my daughters to an event highlighting Dr. King's life or just spending time with my older family members and hearing those stories again about the violence and tragedy of Dr. King's assassination.

During my studying, watching videos and listening to his speeches, I really began to discover who Dr. King was. I looked up to Dr. King. I started to take some of his strongest characteristics and attempt to mirror mine with his. Some of his characteristics were inner strength, courage, Christianity, a powerful orator, a leader and mostly a person who believed passionately in the advancement of people. These are the characteristics I wanted to emulate.

Dr. King's strength is something I've looked up to throughout my life. Dr. King was non-violent, however was met with violence almost daily: dogs attacking him, being called names, rocks thrown at him and finally, a bullet to assassinate him. Even with all those days, months and years of violence Dr. King remained non-violent. I think about the violence Dr. King faced and asked myself if I could have faced such an onslaught and remain non-violent. Initially, my answer was no way. However, I also realized in my own readings and experiences that there was another characteristic that Dr. King had that burns in me... JUSTICE. I have never been attacked by dogs, although some days I had to move into the street so a white person could walk their dog. While I haven't been called names... wait yes, I have been called names like the usual N-word and other disparaging racial epitaphs. While I haven't had rocks thrown at me, I have been told I'm as smart as a box of rocks by my white supervisors. And while I haven't met the bullet of a racist, I have been the victim of injustice like so many others. That led me to pause and think; maybe I do have an inner strength.

Now, courage...this is a tough one. I'm afraid of needles, don't do horror movies and surely don't like any animal with no legs or four legs or as I say it "no legs or fo legs." I had to really think about that over the years when I was faced with some of the similar injustices and how I responded. It takes me back to 1982, Temple Hills, MD, Crossland High School. I was a freshman. Being a freshman was scary enough but one day after school I noticed some white men standing outside passing out leaflets. To my shock and horror, they were recruiting for the local Ku Klux Klan! I wasn't scared, however I made sure my other black friends at the school knew what I saw and we agreed to all walk home together. And this was 1982!

Another example of courage was ironically my freshman year, but this time at the University of Pittsburgh. I remember the predominately white dorm I lived in and how mean my white classmates were. Many of them had never been around articulate or educated blacks but that was no excuse for their behavior. There was a rapist on campus and a picture of the rapist was purposely and maliciously taped to my dormitory door "suggesting" I was the campus rapist. Instead of being scared, I devised a plan to find out which guy it was by telling a classmate I was headed to dinner. When I walked to the elevator, I pretended to push the button as if I was going downstairs, only to say on the floor to see if someone would walk to my door.

Once I knew who it was, I approached this classmate and explained to him, "It takes courage to face you... something you don't have because you couldn't face me." Then I calmly walked away. This was a big day for me because I knew it took courage. He never put anything on my door again about me being the campus rapist.

Dr. King was a Christian above all. He was a preacher and preached the word in church every Sunday. I wasn't in church "every" Sunday but it meant a lot to me to be baptized when I was ten years old. I can still remember how scared I was because I couldn't swim. Reverend Keefer of Hillcrest Baptist Church dipped me into that water and I truly became a believer. Interestingly enough, I said I was a believer but I don't think I really became a believer until some 25 years later, but we will touch on that later. Also, later in the book, I will talk about my time working with an organization called Team Focus. It was at Team Focus that I once again was introduced to the most powerful force in the universe, the Creator...GOD.

Another characteristic that Dr. King had that I wanted to imitate was being a powerful orator. This one, I sort of stumbled across at the age of thirteen. One day I had a terrible cough and sore throat so I stayed home from school, which was very rare for me. I called my mom, who was working at the local grocery store, to ask her a question. The manager answered the phone and said, "Rita, your daughter is on the phone." Well my sister, Kathy was only four years old so my mom knew it must be her son. Something was obviously wrong with my voice. The next day, I woke up and my throat was still sore and the doctor said I needed my tonsils out. This was bad news because I was afraid to have my tonsils taken out. I called my mom at work again to tell her I was afraid and again the manager answered the phone. The manager told my mom, "Rita, I believe it's your husband." Wow, now that's more like it! I liked that and, surprisingly, I also liked the way my voice made the manager move with urgency. I felt powerful... at that moment I knew I had stumbled across something.

Clearly, my voice had changed overnight. I learned that my voice was now deep and rich and when used properly, this new gift from God can help me progress and emulate Dr. King even more. But my tonsils still had to come out...lol.

I never had my tonsils taken out. They are still in and will never come out; remember, I'm afraid of needles. I started reciting Dr. King's speeches. I started copying the President's State of the Union addresses, football coaches' locker room speeches and any other speech I could find. I would make up my own speeches and practice them with my mom's hair brush and make my sister Kathy listen to them over and over. My cousin Kenny loved watching NBA and NFL games with me on television because I would make up my own play by play and colorful commentary. He would marvel as we turned the volume down on the television while I introduced the starting line ups. I noticed I was very articulate and was able to use proper English and grammar, which I knew would take me far...but being a powerful orator would take me far with people who would follow...now that was something I really strived to create, a LEADERSHIP mentality.

Truthfully, I have been a leader since I can remember.

Even at ten years old, I was a boy scout and as soon as the camp director provided an exercise for our troop, I would lead. I remember my first job as a sixteen year old at the local grocery store, sitting in the manager's office when he wasn't there, rocking back in his chair looking down at the sales floor wondering how I could get more out of the employees. I can remember the attempt to start my own fraternity at PITT. I can remember wanting to be the first head coach out of the twenty two in my county to coach college football. Fortunately, I was privileged to lead companies, teams and people in general as an adult. I will detail those experiences a little later in the book.

Lastly, over my lifetime, this is my final King characteristic that I haven't been able to explain or know where it was developed from, but I truly have a passion for the advancement and development of people. This is further evidenced than during time as a leader in my professional life but more as a coach in my personal life. I am Coach Howard! This is who I am and I use football as the vehicle to advance, develop and guide people. You will find football analogies throughout this entire book. Some will make sense, some won't if you aren't a football fan but at the end of the day, my goal is ultimately to advance, develop and help you WIN the game of life. I'm excited and humbled to share some Extra Points with you so you too will win at life.

THE

★ EXTRA POINTS ★

- **THE MOST POWERFUL FORCE IN THE UNIVERSE IS GOD.**

I learned this early and often. If you aren't aware, I could refer you to a bible based church to find out. Prayer is powerful and it works. There is a higher power. Do you believe in miracles? I believe in God. I've seen God work to create the possible when all looks impossible. The first sentence in the bible basically sums up this Extra Point. "In the beginning, God created the heavens and the Earth."

- **LIVING AN ORGANIZED LIFE MEANS KNOWING WHO YOU ARE, WHERE YOU ARE GOING AND HOW YOU ARE GOING TO GET THERE.**

When one speaks of an organized life, it doesn't mean being orderly or having rigid time management, it means you know who you are first. Of course, you want to know your name and where you are from and family traditions etc., but this knowing of who you are is really based more on your core values. It's knowing what you stand for and knowing your purpose in life. Where you are going doesn't mean where you are going to live or your next vacation but where are you taking this life's journey. Are you going to be an author, a playwright, a business person or a missionary? How are you going to get there? Again, this won't be by using a physical road map. This "how" is based on the road you will take in life, the relationships you have along the way and the adversities you overcome to get there.

- **TEAMWORK BEGINS WITH FAMILY.**

As life beats on, it's easy to discover that the first team you will ever play on, count on and love is your family. From the oldest to the youngest, from the nearest to the furthest, family is the first team. Families actually operate similar to sports teams; they eat together, work together, play together, share, cry and celebrate.

Chapter Two

"Let the Games Begin"

For as long as I can remember, football has been woven into my life, in some shape, form or fashion. There's actually a picture of me at five years old, holding a football. It wasn't until I was ten years old that I played on my first team. It was youth football and we actually had a "draft." The draft worked like this; All ten year olds line up. Then you turned your back towards the wall. Then the coaches just said…"give me that one" and someone would tap you on the shoulder and you were on the team. Unfortunately, I had just moved to Camp Springs, Maryland and so I wasn't known in the neighborhood. I kept waiting for the coach to select me but my name wasn't called, nor did anyone tap me on the shoulder. Another kid who was new to the neighborhood was my friend named Wash. Wash was slightly bigger than me and I was skin and bones, but we were about the same size. He was selected by a coach named Mitch. Coach Mitch was the first white man, outside of a teacher, with whom I had ever interacted. He was a middle aged man, with a "dad body." I was really disappointed as I waited and waited for my shoulder to be tapped. Finally, I hear "Keith Howard!" Uh oh…they called my name, now what do I do? The coach told me his name was Mitch and that me and the other new kid, Wash were going to be teammates. Coach Mitch told Wash and I that he would call to provide practice dates, times and locations. I was really excited. Then we received our jerseys. Wow…I had a jersey!

After about a week of waiting, my mom got the call. Practice was the next day. I had no idea what to expect. Watching football on television was one thing but being out on the field was another. I remember thinking this field is so big but before I knew it, practice had started! I didn't know what to expect. Coach Mitch had us line up and we did a lot of jumping jacks. I was so tired. Then, we started running…and running…and running. All this running…I didn't sign up for this. Then Coach Mitch says we have to learn the plays. Learn the plays? I was unsure if I was ready for this…and then the magical moment happened. That kid Washington was really fast…so Coach Mitch said.

"Hey Howard, go block for Washington." I'm thinking to myself...wait I want the ball. The game had begun...life is full of competition.

It was clear the only way I could get in the game and have fun was to block for Washington. The only way I could block for Washington was if I ran as fast as Washington. I did just that...I blocked for Washington. I hoped one day that the coach would put me in the game to run and Washington would block for me for a change. Finally, the coach said, "let's run a reverse...Washington you take the ball and run to the left and then hand the ball to Howard and he will run to the right." I was excited, I'd finally get my chance. And guess what? We scored a touchdown! We just kept running that play and Washington and I were no longer new kids on the block, we were big time stars...at least in our neighborhood.

Back to competition for a moment, the life lesson was exactly that...the only way I could be fulfilled was to compete. In order to compete, I had to prepare. To this day, Coach Wash and I still keep this rule for our running backs...you can't run the ball until you block first.

A few years fly by and the next thing I know I'm in high school. A whole new game begins as high school was a whole new experience. There were several games to be played. Girls, academics, girls, jobs, girls, puberty just to name a few!

Several lessons were learned...I will select academics to show you some of the games played. Elementary school had come very easy for me. I worked really hard. However, like most high school students, I became distracted. The school work was also harder and moved at a faster pace. In tenth grade, I learned a harsh and valuable lesson while playing the game of life. Don't lie because you are going to get caught. I signed up for a data processing class. The class was really difficult. Computers were new and I wasn't very interested in learning this new skill. By the way...I had no idea the internet was right around the corner. I would sit in class and just talk sports the whole time. Me and my friend Quintin Minor would sit in class and talk about our favorite sports teams and didn't really do any school work. Well, fast forward to report card time. The report cards were mailed home and I ran right outside to see my good grades. I opened the mail and I had a "D" in Data Processing. Uh oh…we have a problem. I had never received anything lower than a "C" and my parents were going to be very upset. So what did I do? I decided to just not show them the report card until I changed the grade from a "D" to a "B." Ok, so in my bedroom I go…pencil in hand…just erase a little and fill in with pencil and I'm all good. Oops! I didn't know my own strength and ripped the paper. Now what? Now I'm really in trouble, that's what. A few weeks later, my mom asked…"when are you getting your report card?" I said "the printer broke at school so it will be awhile before we get our report cards." Weeks and weeks went by and I thought my parents had actually forgotten all about my report card. Actually, I know they had forgotten. Then…I got busted. My cousin Erica had been accepted to play women's basketball at the University of Maryland. I bragged all day in school that I was going to see my cousin in her first practice at Maryland. I was getting an early departure from school and everything. My mom stopped by the school to pick me up and asked the office secretary when we were going to get our report cards. The secretary informed my mom that we received our report cards weeks ago. That was the longest seven-minute ride home I had ever had. Needless to say…my butt is still sore from that one. Here's the life lesson though and how damaging a lie can be. While I had to hear and feel the wrath of my parents, I also missed my cousin's big day at the University of Maryland. Those moments are once in a life time and I lost it. That lie also forced me to sort of reestablish my credibility with my parents. From that day on, I feel like I had to prove my integrity to them. The games had really begun.

I will offer one more example of a game to be played. Communications! I never realized how important tone, volume and inflection would be in my life until a day during my "puberty" stage. I called my mom's job and asked to speak to her. The manager said, "Rita, your daughter is on the phone." I was sad that he thought I was a girl. My voice was so high pitched that I sounded like a girl. My sister Kathy was only four years old at the time and wouldn't have been making phone calls yet. I had a really sore throat and mom took me to the doctor. The doctor said I would need my tonsils taken out. I was so afraid of needles so that wasn't happening. Then it happened. The next day I called my mom at work and this time the manager said "Rita, your husband is on the phone." My voice had totally changed! From that day on, not a day goes by that someone doesn't say something about my voice, both positive and negative. Some say how great it sounds, some say it sounds authoritative, some say it doesn't match my body size...my body size? Here's the lesson I learned...communication is such a key to life's game. Over the years, I have learned how to use my voice and all that goes with it...inflection, tone and volume to achieve and progress in the life game. I learned early and often that it is HOW YOU SAY IT. I also learned it's who you say it to.

As my adolescent period began to wind down, I did what most twelfth graders do. I got my first job. I was working at a grocery store where my mom also worked and I had to wear a uniform. I really learned so much from the people who worked there and the customers who shopped there. Most of all, I learned that an honest day's work for an honest day's pay is the way things would be for the next several decades. In order to get to work on time, I took a driving class and passed the driver's license test. In a matter of a few weeks, I was working and driving. I was growing up, and it all was happening so fast.

June 5, 1986 was graduation day. Our class graduated at the Capital Centre which at that time was a state of the art sports arena where the pro basketball and hockey teams played. This was a big deal. I remember it like it was yesterday. Well not exactly because I don't remember who our speaker was at graduation. I do remember, however, the backstage area after graduation. I remember the tears of classmates, as for some, we would never see each other again. Some were going to the military, some already had jobs and were going to work and some like me were going to college. It was the saddest, " happiest" day I had ever had. After the tears, hugs and promises to keep in touch, it was off to the big cookout at my friend Derek's house. My mom even let me borrow her car, a burgundy Volvo four door sedan (and of course I keep Armor All on the tires at all times!) I had so much fun. We danced all night. It's funny because the lesson learned on June 5, 1986 was there is nothing like friendships, especially those you make during your adolescent years. I'm so proud to still keep in touch with so many friends from high school, middle school and yes elementary school. Some of these people have been my friends for over forty eight years. Little did I know then what I know now, which is treat people well because you never know when you may need them.

Through my teen years, I noticed that the game of life had really begun. Those games during the fundamental years were valuable learning experiences. The funny part is the game continues through your teen and formative years all the way to adulthood. To me, there's been no more transformative decade than ten to twenty years old. People ask the question, if you had it to do all over again what would you change? Well during these years, I wouldn't change a thing. I had fun. I was a kid who grew into a young man. You have to know that maturity is a process. Physically I was a late bloomer, but mentally I was a sponge that soaked up information and grew. I have such fond memories of my childhood. Nothing is more comforting then being able to pick up the phone and reach out to an old friend. Seeing them now, fully mature, wise and prospering is great. As an adult, especially in tough times, it was those memories, those relationships and those times that always brought a smile to my face. During these years, I truly didn't have a care in the world. There was no internet, no social media and barely cable television and we still found a way to stay connected. Life was simple. As I watch my own children now, I feel like life is really complicated. Turn on the news sometimes and listen to the world and how challenging a world it is. Social media has Throwback Thursday in which people post pictures of themselves during a past decade. I wish this was a week long holiday where everything was a throwback. Throwing back to a simpler time when the world was a kinder, gentler place.

Unfortunately, as the games begin, they also change. With each year, added responsibilities dictate the game and the players. In my early elementary school days, I didn't have a care in the world. I went to school, came home, did homework, played in the snow and played outside all day and night in the summer. Then in my teen years, things started to get serious. I had a job. I discovered girls. All of a sudden, I had to start making decisions, major decisions. Then in young adulthood came independence and even bigger decisions. Of course, there's parenthood…that's a whole new ball of wax. Talk about a game changer…

parenthood is it! Fortunately, I have been able to win the games of life. This is exactly what Extra Points is all about…WINNING. Winning in the game of life and making sure that your life has a story to be told.

THE

★ EXTRA POINTS ★

- **THE FRIENDSHIPS MADE DURING ADOLESCENT YEARS ARE VERY SPECIAL.**

Friendships in general are so important and so special. However, I notice over time that the ones that are really lifelong and everlasting are the friendships made during the adolescent years. These years are the formative years. Think about it…puberty, prom, graduation, driver's license, first job, clubs and organizations, first date, sweet sixteen, etc. With the onset of social media, look at the number of reunions that pop up, both formal and informal. As I wrote this book, I so enjoyed the memories of these relationships. The adult relationships are great too but there's innocence and a charm to adolescence.

- **MATURITY IS A PROCESS.**

When I was a teen and my mom would say "you are acting immature", I thought nothing of it. Matter of fact, I thought she was the one that was immature. Now that I'm forty seven and have two daughters on the other side of their teen years, I see what mom meant. Once I reached the twenty something's age, I thought I had matured. Nope! Not at all, not even close…I was so immature even then.

Ok…thirties? Not really…maturity hit me in my late thirties. Maturity is a process. Basically you have to live life first. You have to fail. You have to succeed. You have to live. Maturity takes time. You will know when it hits you…when you have matured.

- **AS LIFE'S GAMES BEGIN, THEY ALSO CONTAIN MANY A TWIST AND TURN.**

The game of life is like any other game. I can remember some football games I coached where there were so many twists and turns and intangibles that no matter how much I prepared, I just wasn't ready. There's a phrase said on the football field "keep your head on a swivel." It means look around, stay alert, keep your eyes open, watch your back, etc. This is because you never know when someone (the opponent) or maybe even a teammate or referee may run right into you and could cause injury. Life works the same way. You just don't know when, how, who or where life's twists and turns will come calling in your world. The extra point here is to always prepare for as much as you can but realize you can't control all things. Sometimes in life you just have to roll with the punches… at least you know there will be punches.

- **IN ORDER TO LIVE FULFILLED LIVES, AT SOME POINT YOU MUST COMPETE.**
In all things there is competition and competition is healthy. Competition brings out the best in everyone. Competition starts early in life at school. We compete through our academics for scholarships and for advancement for a better quality of life. Depending on where our life travels take us we compete in our workplace. We compete for the jobs.

We compete for the promotions. We compete for the business. We compete in love. Competing is like comparing to something else and trying to outperform the establishment or incumbent. The extra point here is to compete early and often and win.

• **DON'T LIE...YOU ARE GOING TO GET CAUGHT.**

Proverbs 12:22 says "lying lips are an abomination to the Lord." We know that as believers if it's in the Bible then it's true. However, unfortunately we all have been there. We all have lied and we all have been caught. Now, some of us haven't been "caught" and think we get away with lying however God sees and knows everything. If you ever wonder why things aren't going your way...see if you lied lately. I bet that's why. Tell the truth. It may hurt but lying hurts more. The extra point here is an age old adage "honesty is the best policy."

"Extra Points"

Chapter Three

"Reaching a Cross Land"

Everybody has a story or a dream…you have one, I have one, we all have one. From the beginning, mine was to be a Head Football Coach. While at the University of Pittsburgh, I had a bird's eye view of big time college program. It was my dream job. Unfortunately, I also saw the politics of getting that job, especially if you were a black male, but I will come back to that shortly. While at PITT, I followed my old high school team closely. Now, Crossland High School was never a power house in football. In my senior year, the basketball team won the school's only state championship. The football team was traditionally a hard-nosed 5-5 team. The team really only had two wildly successful coaches in its history, John Merrick and Larry Layman. Coach Layman was the coach while I attended Crossland. Coach Layman was an amazing man. He had been at the school since the 1960s. His battles with nearby Friendly High School were legendary. Coach Layman and Coach Merrick were the school's all-time winning coaches. Coach Layman decided to retire in the early 90's. I thought that with my experience, I would be the perfect replacement. I had what few coaches had in our county…college coaching experience. I visited the school and noticed it was very different from when I was a student in the late 80s. The demographics had changed. The school was now majority black. The academics had decreased. The career tech wing was all but deserted. The suspension rate was through the roof. When I visited the school to drop off my resume, I was told that one of Coach Layman's assistants would probably get the job. I was shocked!

Paul Cherrier was named Head Football Coach at Crossland. I reached out to Coach Cherrier and told him I was an alum and wanted to help out. Coach Cherrier gave me an opportunity as a Junior Varsity Coach. I told him I had a guy who could coach offense named Tim Washington. Coach Wash…my old classmate and I were getting our second coaching gig together at Crossland! We made an immediate impact. I can remember the Head Junior Varsity Coach, Desi Brown, basically letting us run the team. Coach Wash was the offensive coordinator and I did the defense and special teams. We went 8-0. The varsity went 2-8. Towards the tail end of the year, Coach Cherrier asked me and Coach Wash to start helping on varsity. We received a chilly reception from the other varsity coaches as we came in very collegial and clearly with a different mindset. In the off-season, I spoke to Coach Cherrier about being on varsity the following season. Coach Cherrier, however, had news for me. He was resigning after one season. With Coach Cherrier moving to Vermont to take another opportunity, I thought "here's a window to become Head Coach." I worked my tail off. Numerous letters of recommendations from college coaches, conference commissioners and even NFL players (my old PITT buddies) were flowing into Crossland High School. After interviewing on a cold snowy night in January, and after waiting for months, I found out that I didn't get the job. I was pretty bummed. I told Coach Wash, let's take our show on the road. Crossland was in a league that was on the decline. We needed to strengthen our resume.

I remembered my sister attending Bishop Ireton

High School, and I wondered what their coaching needs were. It was a private school in northern Virginia. I met the football coach. His name was Chip Armstrong. Chip was a great guy and really educated me on how the private school leagues were a real resume builder. A few months went by and Coach Armstrong was named Head Football Coach at Bishop McNamara High School. Bishop McNamara was a private school in my county. They played powerhouse DeMatha Catholic High School every year and they sent hundreds of student-athletes to college on football scholarships. I stopped by McNamara and asked Coach Armstrong if he needed help. He offered me another Junior Varsity position. I wasn't interested in that at all but it got my foot in the door. We had a great year on Junior Varsity and like Crossland, I started helping out the varsity. The next season, I was named QB's coach. I knew nothing about coaching QB's but I did know a former NFL offensive coordinator, Paul Hackett. I watched Coach Hackett tutor Quarterbacks at PITT so I had tons of drills. It wasn't the drill work that made me successful, it was teaching quarterbacks how to be great leaders. I was a coach who taught leadership. I also learned clock management, poise and offensive play calling.

However, here's what I didn't learn at PITT…how to deal with parents…let me explain! We had three quarterbacks at McNamara. We had the senior drop back passer, the athletic option quarterback and the freshman who just had all the intangibles. The senior and the freshman were brothers so that made this more difficult. I thought the freshman should have played. One of the things I learned at PITT, you always play the best players. The freshman was the best player. We muddled through the season playing all three and ending up with an early out in the league playoffs. Once again, a coaching change as Coach Armstrong left to coach at another school in Baltimore.

Coach Bernard Joseph who was our defensive coordinator was selected as the new Head Football Coach at Bishop McNamara and he too was a great guy. Coach Joseph was an alum of McNamara and I liked that he was back to help his school. Meanwhile, across town at Crossland, the team was posting loss after loss. The team was finishing last in the standings and I was watching. I can remember going to a Crossland game and standing in the rain watching my old school get killed. I could vision how I could bring them back to prominence. McNamara became frustrating as it appeared as though public school coaches were somewhat overlooked when it came to game planning and strategy. I can remember informing Coach Joseph that I was going to be a Head Coach someday.

After two frustrating years, I decided to take an interesting move…leave McNamara and go back to a public school. My other coaching friends were asking me if I was crazy? Here I am at a private school with college opportunities swirling around and I'm leaving to go back to the place that some say was holding me back? Yes! I had a plan. With Crossland struggling mightily…I had come to a crossroads. I needed to get the attention of the school that they needed to make a change to me. I also wanted to coach in the public schools because I saw the difference in the family nucleus and wanted to help develop the public school athlete.

During the off-season, I decided to apply at every high school in my county that had an opening. I applied at five different schools and received five letters saying "Thanks but no thanks." I wasn't sure why I couldn't get a high school head job. I had so much to offer. I called an old coaching colleague named Ed Shields. Coach Shields was the Head Football Coach at Northwestern High School. I explained to Coach Shields that I needed to coach against Crossland. Crossland was one of the worst teams in the state by this point and he didn't understand why this was important to me. I told him "Coach just let me coach defense." Fast forward to homecoming at Northwestern High School. That week…I wore every Crossland tee shirt I had to a Northwestern practice. I explained to everyone that by wearing the tee-shirt, I was reminding them that we needed to destroy this team. Yes…I was going to put my own school out to pasture in order to get the head coaching job and return it back to relevance. This game was played in 2000. Still Coach Shields and any player I see today quote the speech I gave in the locker room just prior to kickoff. I can remember the passion and tears I shed during that locker room speech. We beat Crossland 71 to 0 that day. After the game, I went to the Principal at Crossland and said "Hi, I'm your new head football coach." Within a few months of interviews, politics and just plain old wrangling…in March of 2003, I was finally named Head

Football Coach at Crossland High School.

First order of business, hire Coach Wash! Yall remember Coach Wash? Coach Washington (Wash) was the young man that I played football with when I was younger. Second order of business was to meet the players. Third order of business...well, win a game! Not to mention the in-school suspension was established during my first year as Head Football Coach at Crossland High School. The in-school suspension classroom size was larger than the average classroom, so I need to address this as well.

I remember the first game like it was yesterday... a 28-0 loss to Duval. I wasn't nervous. I was born to do this. I decided during summer training camp to play the seniors who had lost the majority of their games over their career and keep the freshman on junior varsity and out of harm's way. We lost every game by at least 30 points and brought the Crossland winless streak to 19 games in a row. I had a plan. The plan was in writing and I stayed with it. I can remember playing our arch rival - Friendly High school in a game in which their quarterback who now starts for the Cleveland Browns beat us 50 to 14. If that wasn't enough...3 of my players went to the hospital during that game due to injury. I can remember a game in Delaware. We lost but were happy we just scored over 20 points. I started doing some things that were in the plan, for instance, having college coaches come around more for recruiting, have Friday night dinners with our parents and established a study hall and weight lifting program. While the scores were lopsided, each week we were getting better; the problem was I was the only one to see it. Finally, season one is over. The young players can now move up to varsity.

First things first, get them out of their losing environment. I changed the scenery and took the twenty best players to my old stomping grounds…PITT football. Coach Wash and I organized the whole weekend. The players competed and saw that in Pittsburgh there's a higher level of commitment to football. We didn't play well and that was ok…what we did do was grow in 72 hours. We ate together, told stories and bonded. That's what this team needed. In season two, we won our first game on the last play of the game. The crowd went crazy. We went on to win our first three in a row. However, with only about 30 players and injuries mounting and just being young, we finished with a 4-6 record. The progress made year three a highly anticipated adventure. Again, my team was a year older.

Sadly, I noticed that many of my players were growing up without a father. This was making the job even tougher. In most cases, I was the first male who cared and showed how much I cared by growing them up to be a man first and a football player second. We were headed back to PITT for summer camp, but this time we finished our season and immediately got in the weight room. We also finished strong in the classroom. Again, we traveled back to PITT. This time the trip was much different on the field. We were competing and confidence was growing. My quarterback, Andre Taylor, was one of those players who were growing up "without a dad." He was a real struggle for me. I called Coach Gottfried, who I hadn't spoken to since our last day at PITT in December 1989. Coach Gottfried told me about Team Focus. Team Focus is a nonprofit that caters to young males without fathers. He and I caught up and he was happy to hear I was a Head Football Coach. I told him about Andre. Coach Gottfried suggested putting him in Team Focus. It worked! Andre was leading our team.

In year three, we still hadn't quite turned the corner and finished 3-7. Year four was upon us. The parents were still supportive but I could feel the heat. I was failing on the field; however I had graduated at least fifteen players off to college football or the military. We started off slow. I was starting to feel even more pressure.

One day in practice, Andre and another player who was also in Team Focus (Robert Allen) got into a fight. This was a big deal. They were both captains and in Team Focus and were as close to being coaches on the field as possible. Unfortunately, I benched them both. I played a younger player (Terrance Manago) at quarterback. I can remember the local newspaper writing an article on my decision. I can remember a fan (Phil White) in the stands booing me to no end. The decision to bench my two cornerstones of the team lit a flame with my players. Crossland went on to win five straight games, something that hadn't been done since Coach Layman retired and hasn't been done since I resigned in 2007.

Finally, after an 8-2 regular season, it all came down to a coin toss. Yes, for the first time in Maryland state history…a coin toss was going to decide the final playoff spot. That means…three other playoff tiebreakers still led to a tie. It was Crossland and Bowie…finally Crossland is relevant again! After years of losing, Crossland was a coin toss away. I can remember the week of the toss and the media attention was incredible. Everywhere I went, people were asking "heads or tails" which brought me to a life lesson…we all have choices, however sometimes those choices are out of our hands and out of our control. I remember telling our players that week about choices. Some of them were making college choices, some were making other bigger choices like what to do after graduation.

Choices…we all have them. This coin toss was a choice. Heads or tails...life is a little more complicated. Life has so many choices every single day. As we grow, the choices become more complicated, more important and yet they are still just choices. I would rather have them than not have them…I just try to make the most of them. The night before the coin toss, I made my choice. Tails never fails so I was picking tails. I went to bed and had a dream that I was washing my hair. That made me change my mind when I woke up to pick heads instead of tails. Well little did I know…this had never happened in the history of Maryland secondary school athletics and the rules weren't quite what I had anticipated. First of all, the coin toss was held in a hotel…yes in a hotel. There were cameras and media there. Both coaches were there and briefed that the ruling is the schools were put in alphabetical order and the school that is alphabetically first is heads and the other is tails. Unfortunately for me, I couldn't pick heads…I had to stay with tails due to the rules. After what seemed like an hour of rules and administrative stuff, out comes the coin. Everything else was in slow motion. The state official walked out slowly and put the coin in his hands. He showed us the coin one last time. I remember like yesterday…the coin flipped over and over and dropped on the floor. Cameras were flashing. You could hear a pin drop in the room. HEADS! The official yelled and our hopes were crushed. I called Coach Wash to give him the news and told him I would announce it tomorrow at school. The players were anticipating the announcement and had their stomach in knots. I took that night to think about what I was going to say to my players.

Robert Allen, a captain, had the best grades. Robert

was thinking about attending Randolph Macon. Andre Taylor, also a captain, was thinking about many different colleges but didn't have the grades Robert had. I had twenty seven players that year and twelve were seniors. All of them had choices and the announcement I was about to make was going to accelerate their decisions, and change their lives.

There was tension in the school all day that day. I arrived at my usual time of 1:30pm. I called a team meeting in the gym for immediately after school. Everyone gathered. I began by telling them who made the all-star team for the year. We had six all-stars that year, more than Crossland had in the previous ten years combined. I announced that I would be the Head Coach of the South All-Star team. Then it was the moment of truth…I talked to the players about choices. I told them that we all have choices and some are beyond our control and some are in our control. This coin toss was out of our control but the work we do as the result of the coin toss can determine so much more. I told the team with tears in my eyes…"We lost the coin toss." The team was devastated, especially those seniors. The assistant coaches did a great job of consoling the players. This was the toughest loss I had ever experienced in coaching. I had no idea losing could be this painful. I thought about resigning.

I took the off-season to work on getting those seniors in school. Robert Allen went to Randolph-Macon and played football there. Andre Taylor went on to play junior college football in Mississippi and Alabama. I returned to coach one more season at Crossland but things weren't the same. While the junior class who played on the coin toss team had a good season, it just wasn't the same. I was tired. The number of interviews just to get the job, the number of losses, the number of players injured during the lean years, the disapproval of fans, the side eyes from even the janitors, just the whole thing…I was tired. I coached that last season hard but my aspirations for bigger and better were on my mind. I was reaching a "cross land" full of choices. I love my school. I wear my class ring every day as it's the first thing I bought with my own money. I keep in touch with many of my high school friends.

My first choice after my final season at Crossland was to return to a college football sideline as an assistant coach at The Catholic University of America. I've made many choices in my life and they all lead back to just another "cross land."

Today, I'm still telling the story of the "coin toss" to audiences all over the country. Life is just a coin toss some time; you win and sometimes you lose.

THE
★ EXTRA POINTS ★

- **EVERYBODY HAS A STORY.**

I first heard this phrase from my old ball coach Mike Gottfried at the University of Pittsburgh. Basically, what Coach Gottfried was referencing was we all truly do have a story and the story is for good. Every interaction, every experience is part of our story. The question is do YOU know what your story is and can you tell it? The Extra Point is that everybody has a story and every person has value.

- **PERSEVERE FOR YOUR PASSION.**

The Extra Point is just a reminder that while you are chasing and achieving your passion you will have obstacles and setbacks in the way. In order to reach your passion you must persevere. Meet every challenge and work through it, around it or over it. In order to have something of any worth, you must persevere. The Extra Point here is to figure out how, who and what can you do, to accomplish the mission of reaching your passion.

- **WE ALL HAVE CHOICES SOMETIMES THE OUTCOMES ARE OUT OF OUR CONTROL.**

The Extra Point is there are choices in every situation. Think about the first five minutes of your day. Upon waking up, you have so many choices. Turn off the alarm and go back to bed, get up immediately, eat breakfast, exercise, go to work, what to wear, etc. etc. etc. Fact of the matter is while we all have choices some of the outcomes are out of our control. For example, if you choose to eat breakfast but the local restaurant is closed due to bad weather then the choice of eating breakfast is still in your hands but the outcome of going out for breakfast is out of your control since the restaurant decided to close. You may choose to apply for a job and never hear back from the company you applied too. The outcome is out of your control because the company may have decided not to fill the position or fill in with an internal candidate. The Extra Point here is we do all have choices and yes some of them are out of our control but don't lose YOUR control because God is truly in control.

- **LIFE IS JUST A COIN TOSS SOMETIMES YOU WIN AND SOMETIMES YOU LOSE.**

When you flip a coin it either lands heads or tails, well life works the same way. Life is all about timing and not the timing on your watch. Life is all about God's timing. You may make a left turn and stumble on the love of your life. You may make a right turn and lose your life in a car accident. In life sometimes you win sometimes you lose. Enjoy and embrace the wins and learn and grow from the losses.

- **MAKE YOUR LIFE PLANS SPECIFIC, MEASURABLE, ACHIEVABLE, REALISTIC AND TIME SENSITIVE.**

Every life project, no matter how big or small, is easily achieved if it has a plan. This SMART plan is one of many ways to ensure you have a starting point. By making the plan very specific, you will stay focused on the prize at hand, which is completion of the goal. Measuring the progress also helps you to decide whether or not you need to make changes and/or adjustments within the plan. Working a plan that isn't achievable can be very frustrating, so why start there? Give yourself every opportunity to succeed. Make sure the plan is achievable and realistic. Finally, put a timeline on this goal. This keeps you on track and gives you something to continue to chase especially when you start to tire.

Chapter Four

"In the PITT"

April 3, 1986…Coach Wash (who was Tim back then) and I had a trip planned to visit the University of Pittsburgh. We rode the train. Longest ride I've ever taken and during the ride, while we were really excited to be away from home and everything, I knew this was going to be tough. Tough like this isn't the comforts of home… it was April and there was still snow on the ground. It was cold. We stopped in every little town like Altoona, Pennsylvania and saw people who looked like they were just tough. I had heard of the steel city but seeing it up close and personal was different. When we arrived in Pittsburgh for our visit, I noticed people looking at us funny like we were different. Then it hit me…I asked Wash… "what is that funky smell?" Wash said, "I don't know but it stinks" and that's when we named the sulfur and iron ore mix of the closed down steel mills…"the stink." From just the smell alone, I knew there was no way I could attend here…but then we arrived at our hotel and I thought maybe I can. The hotel was called the University Club. I noticed people staring at us again and I felt different. Still the new experience overshadowed "the stink" and we were excited to be in the Pitt. We stayed a few days in Pittsburgh and we liked it. I think we liked the independence more than anything so we decided to attend the University of Pittsburgh.

I remember prior to school starting visiting PITT Stadium. Wow…what an awesome site. You walk nearly straight up a hill to get to the stadium. At the top of the hill PITT Stadium and the new football coach Mike Gottfried sat. Coach Gottfried had just come from Kansas University and was moving up the coaching ranks. Immediately, I knew this is where I wanted to be. I saw an ad in the PITT NEWS for a student manager. I knew nothing about being a manager but knew it would give me a bird's eye view of things. Wash and I still couldn't shake off this feeling of how we were looked at, spoken to, or treated by the majority white student body. Wash and I were from DC. We had all the sense of purpose, style and arrogance DC had to offer. Maybe that was it? Maybe that's why we were getting these funny looks…then it hit us. We were feeling this way because we aren't liked. Dare we say the "R" word? Now that I'm older and have experienced more…I know that racism exists. However, at eighteen years old, I didn't know what it looked like at all. One day after a long day full of classes, Wash and I discovered a picture from the PITT NEWS taped to our door. There was a rapist on campus and someone wrote on the picture that the rapist was me! That is when Wash and I coined a phrase that's used all the time now…"subtle racism."

Subtle racism is disguised, covert; it's not public or obvious racism. It is the sort of racism that discriminates against individuals through often unnoticeable or seemingly passive methods. Subtle racism is often racially biased decisions hidden or rationalized with an explanation that is more acceptable by society.

There are too many examples of subtle racism in our country today. Things like our prison system, racial profiling, the inequalities of health care and access to affordable housing and education, just to name a few. Wash and I used to compare notes on how "subtle racism" affected us on a given day. For example, if we walked, the white students would jump out of the way even though they weren't in the way and say excuse me or sorry. Wash and I would look at each other like this is crazy. They would put their heads down when we walked by them. If, however, our back was turned, they would do something like put a picture of a rapist on our door. They would say little things like…"you don't like fried chicken?" This was something new for us to tolerate. Wash walked around the dorm with a bat and me with a weightlifting belt. Not sure what I was going to do with the weightlifting belt but I sure felt tough. We were little trail blazers and didn't even know what we were going to blaze. Let's move on.

It's my first day in my new job as student manager for the PITT Football team. My primary job that year was to do the most humiliating things imaginable. Pick up dirty jock straps, clean up after grown football players' lockers, pick up dirty towels and wash them, hand out clean socks and the list goes on forever. I also had to learn how to fix equipment which I had no clue how to do. Practice was hard. In the winter, practice started at 4am in the morning. If you were late, you were in big trouble as our job was to be there prior to the players and coaches arriving and leave after they leave. Only one problem, at 4am in Pittsburgh, it's very dark and very cold. Wash was triple jumping for PITT and I told him "hey man…they pay some of your tuition and feed you." A few weeks later, Wash joined me. We sort of made a deal then…"learn everything we can and someday become coaches ourselves." One of my main points of emphasis in my new job was to take care of the new coach. Make sure he is outfitted; make sure he has bubble gum, a jacket, and a hat, anything he needed.

During this time, I got to know Coach Gottfried pretty well. I could anticipate what he needed, how he was feeling, what he wanted and really who he is and what it takes to be a head coach of a big time college football program. Now back to the subtle racism thing…Wash and I noticed that out of ten student managers, only the two of us had such an up close and personal look at PITT Football through the lenses of the coaching staff. Then we noticed that we weren't allowed to travel with the team for our first road game. We were treated like we were walk-on players. Now don't get me wrong, there were older guys ahead of us but we worked just as hard as they did. We worked harder than some players. We worked all the hours. That season we went 8-3 including a big win over Penn State. This job was great because we were learning with some of the brightest coaches in college football. Some of the coaches we worked with are still coaching in the NFL.

I learned something from every great coach that was there. John Harbaugh…I learned special teams is very important. Coach Harbaugh was a special team wiz for the Philadelphia Eagles prior to becoming Head Coach of the Baltimore Ravens. Mike McCarthy…you may have to work a job just to keep your dream going. Coach McCarthy worked a full-time job at night, then came to practice during the day. Coach McCarthy is now the Head Coach of the Green Bay Packers. John Fox…who told me once after practice while walking off the field…" Always play the best player…always." Speaking of John Fox, he also taught me the importance of urgency. One day during training camp, I was running the scout team. The scout team are walk on players who "day in and day out "run the opponents plays to get the scholarship athletes ready for the next game. I got tired of seeing these players who worked hard get no acknowledgment or recognition. Plays were drawn on cards back then and the scout team would run those plays. The defense would destroy the walk-ons. The next play was designed to run right but I decided to throw left. Coach Fox was fuming. He said "Howard, I will rip your lips off and send you back to DC…don't ever do that again." I was like, wow, this guy was really upset. But I learned a lesson. Coach Fox is now the Head Coach of the Chicago Bears.

I had no idea how much went into three hours of my life on Saturday afternoons in the fall. Our schedule was so busy. I was rarely in my dorm or library. I was at PITT Stadium working in the PITT. After a few average seasons and above average recruiting classes, the coaching bug was really apparent. I started spending all my time upstairs with the coaches. Listening, sharing and soaking up every aspect of running a big time collegiate program. I saw the good and the not so good. The good was how gracious Coach Gottfried was with his players but he was also gracious with just everyday people. Here he is, the Head Football Coach for the University of Pittsburgh taking time out for children with special needs or just a homeless person on the street. I saw the bad. Wash and I were the lowest paid out of the other student managers. We had to earn respect and earn everything that was given to us. I saw how losing can take its toll on a coach and how winning is rarely enjoyed. I saw how "subtle racism" is played in big time college athletics just like it was in my dorm room. Yet, I couldn't help imagining this would be me someday leading a college football team.

I do have some great memories. My most wonderful memory actually was beating Penn State at home and then again at Penn State. During the week at practice, Coach Fox had a great game plan. He was our Defensive Coordinator and kept preaching certain looks the Penn State offense would give. With Penn State driving as we hang on to a slim lead, our Strong Safety, Billy Owens steps in front of a pass and streaks down the side line. I raced down the sideline with him. I saw the game on replay one night and can still quote the play by play!

Then I have some "not great memories." The low light for me was the day Coach Gottfried got fired. PITT had signed him to a lifetime contract. For four years, I followed this man's every move, every step and every word. Coach Gottfried was instilling and shaping me, not just for the coach I am today but the man I am today. I learned so many valuable lessons from this transaction. I learned that you coach until you get fired. I learned that it's better to work smart AND hard. I learned to value and treasure every relationship.

Wow, did we make some relationships...like Coach Gottfried...I liked the little guy. The guy no one even cares about or even notices what they do. I just wanted to take a moment to shout out a few...Walt and Sincan and all the maintenance men at PITT Stadium. These guys knew everything. They would always pull me and Wash to the side and just give us some wisdom. They were the little guy who did big things. I never knew how important the field operations were. Now, I'm a field operations guru. Les Banos was our video guy. Video was still cutting and clipping 8mm tape. As we were going to a more digital feel for video, Les was way ahead of his time. Jesse Long and Ray Goga...they protected Coach Gottfried. I never knew how important security was until observing these guys. They also were good at stuff like hotel logistics, finding stadiums as there was no Google maps back then. There were so many people and so many coaches who taught me so much. Shout out to those guys and so many more.

Now, let's return back to Coach Gottfried. I can remember it like it was yesterday. Things were getting heated around the football program. We had recruited the best high school football players in the nation for two years but only had 14 wins to show for it. After a mess of a bowl game, in which we lost on the field and the bowl went bankrupt, the pressure to win was really on everyone. With wins over power house programs like Ohio State, Notre Dame and Penn State, there were losses to Temple, domination by Syracuse and battles with Navy and Boston College. It was a game in Dublin, Ireland versus Rutgers over Thanksgiving weekend that would prove to be the beginning of the end. We lost the game, however, during halftime, as the coaches were making adjustments, the Mayor of Pittsburgh at the time, Sophie Masloff, had some sort of press conference or something. This didn't sit well with Coach Gottfried.

I knew that once we were back in Pittsburgh, there were going to be repercussions from this whole trip. I was right. Coach Gottfried had signed a lifetime contract, however, in early December 1989, the news broke…PITT was going in a different direction and that would not include my coach.

I sat back and just observed. I saw and learned so many things. First, I learned if you coach long enough you will be fired. It's part of the job. Second, being a Head Coach or a leader of anything for that matter is very lonely. As we were all walking around in a fog, it was also announced that we had to prepare for a bowl game. We were playing Texas A&M in a matter of weeks. I was excited. While I had traveled the country thanks to football, this trip was different. This trip was without Mike Gottfried. Paul Hackett, our offensive coordinator, took over the team. I can remember those coaches and staff who were so loyal to Coach Gottfried having to slowly transition to a new voice. I was only 21 years old. I wasn't mature enough to even think about the ripple effect this transition would have on staff that now would probably need to find other jobs. This family was being blown up right before my young eyes. It did affect me as well. While Coach Hackett was being announced by school President, Wesley Posvar, as PITT's new Head Football Coach, moments before we took the field at the John Hancock Sun Bowl, a letter was being mailed to my house letting me know my athletic scholarship would not be renewed. Coach Gottfried disappeared. I was really sad. It is funny how life works and who comes into your life and who makes an impact.

During those four years at PITT, Mike Gottfried made the most positive impact in my life. Those years were the toughest I had ever experienced. I had always received good grades from kindergarten until graduation from high school. However, at PITT I struggled academically. I attended summer school all four years. I didn't always apply myself but even when I did I struggled. During my adolescence, I've always had the basics. Food, water and shelter...however at PITT there were times when I didn't have food water and shelter. One semester, I decided to go back to PITT and try to make it without my football scholarship or my parents help. My parents and I had a disagreement and I left home. I used a bag of pennies saved up since childhood to board the bus and head to PITT. Wow...did I learn how hard life can be. Once I went 76 hours without food and I saw a man bite into a hamburger and then throw it in the trash. I was so hungry I reached in the trash can and pulled the half eaten burger out and ate it. Times were hard for me.

I also experienced adversity that I hadn't quite

encountered before emotionally. I met a young lady at PITT who I cared about a lot and she cared about me. The difficulty came in, because she was of a different race. Interracial dating in Pittsburgh was a real challenge in the 1980's. We were denied service at restaurants, stared at, heckled, because we were different. Overtime, due to outside influences, the relationship became toxic. It put a real strain on me as well as my parents. The young lady explained to me that her family would be very disappointed if they found out about our relationship. Consequently, my parents couldn't understand why or how I could date someone whose family wasn't accepting of me. Along with the emotional strain, the relationship also took a physical toll as well. Things started to get worse during the relationship. During another violent argument, she went to slam the door in my face and I stuck my hand in the door. OUCH! My finger needed stitches. Ironically, I was recently off my parent's health care, I refused to go to the emergency room. I had to ask Wash the improbable. I asked him to stitch my hand with hot needle and thread. Consequently, I still have that scar today. Finally, after years of an on again off again relationship we ended our relationship. It was heartbreaking, for both of us.

Tough times continued. While staying in an off-campus apartment owned by a slum lord. We noticed it was unusually cold in the apartment even for Pittsburgh weather. The heat wasn't working. We decided to stop paying rent. The landlord continued to say he would fix the heat. Meanwhile, we are freezing. In order to make sure we weren't evicted, we decided to pay our rent to an escrow account. The health department told us we had to monitor the temperature for thirty days. During those thirty days, the average temperature in our apartment was twenty-two degrees. One night, Wash and I were studying and were really exhausted. We were pulling a college all night cram session. As the wee hours of the morning was upon us, I told Wash I needed some heat and I was going to turn on the gas stove for heat. Wash warned me that I could die of carbon monoxide poisoning if I fell asleep. I heard him but my eyes were closing. As I slowly drifted off to sleep, Wash stayed awake and watched my chest go up and down to make sure I was alright. I only took a quick cat nap before he woke me up. I realized this guy just made sure I was living. As his Calculus book started to slowly slip out of his hands, I did the same thing for him. As his chest went up and down, I watched him closely. After a few short minutes of shut eye, I woke Wash up too. We did this all night, and finished our studying. We made it through but barely.

Today, I share with my daughters that those days of walking in the cold, going without food and really just being on my own was the greatest education of all. I learned more outside of the classroom than in it. All of these adversities taught me so much more than the classroom ever did. I was in the PITT. Now as a grown adult, I love my school and cherish those memories both good and bad. When my youngest daughter applied to PITT, it warmed my heart. When my oldest daughter asked me to take her to see Arianna Grande in concert on PITT's campus, I was full of warm memories and had come full circle. My visits now are nostalgic. I've returned for football, for work and even to just get away and clear my head and remind myself how far I have come in life. I love PITT. Beat Penn State. Hail to PITT!

THE

★ EXTRA POINTS ★

- **IF YOU WORK/COACH LONG ENOUGH, YOU WILL BE FIRED AND YOU WILL REBOUND.**

We all get fired. This Extra Point is to all those who haven't gotten fired yet. It will happen IF you work long enough. I clearly have seen this, especially in the coaching field where they actually have a term called "Black Monday" in which coaches get fired the Monday after the NFL regular season. There are websites created just to be able to track the comings and goings of fired coaches. Terminations aren't pleasant. Having experienced it more than once in my life, I can tell you it is a painful, lonely feeling. However, the good thing about terminations is the old saying, "when one door closes, the other door opens" and usually it's an upgrade. Just remember...all you can do is control what you can control. Work hard and always prepare for the next job.

- **ADVERSITY BUILDS CHARACTER.**

A simple Extra Point is adversity builds character. In its simplicity, it may also be the truest statement imaginable. In order to find out who you really are, you must have some adversity in your life. Adversity brings out the absolute best in you. Disappointments like broken hearts, financial issues, health related matters, etc., can humble you to a point of tearing out the real who in you. I think about a few of my adversities…I lost $15M dollars yet my character makes me richer than I've ever been. My heart's been broken more than one time yet I love God and love others including myself. I've been fired and happy about it because the next door was always greener. Adversity has also strengthened my faith. Sometimes, when you go through life and all is well, you can forget to count your blessings, but if you been through adverse times…you will never ever forget to count your blessings.

- **YOU MAKE YOUR BED HARD, YOU LAY HARD.**

Another simple Extra Point is common sense. If you make it difficult, it will be difficult. For example, if you stay up late and have to get up early, you will be dreading it the next morning. If you spend your money and don't save, you will find that rainy day fund hard to come by. I've made my bed hard so many times I have fire logs for pillows. When I went to lie in that bed I got splinters and it wasn't comfortable at all. I try my best to make my bed every day. When I make that bed, I try to make it with cotton linen that's so soft so when the day is over and I want to just jump in the bed…there will be a soft landing.

Chapter Five

"The $15M Fumble"

June 1996 – I'm working my corporate America job at a large financial institution. I was employee of the year my last two years with the bank. All was well in the world...I was growing and learning. I was learning from the best in the business too. I worked in a Private Banking/Trust & Investment Center . The team assembled was the best at what they did for other banks, and now we were all together. I was the youngest of the bunch and just soaked up the experiences like a sponge. Then one random day, my dad calls and offers me an opportunity to join the family business. I was happy because my dad had built a large security company. He had hired thousands of security guards to protect government buildings all over the DC area. This was an impressive feat as I remember the company started just as I had graduated from Crossland High School and was leaving for PITT. One day, my dad decided to quit his comfortable government job to start a security company just as I was about to leave for college? Honestly, I thought to myself, "what in the world is he thinking?" My dad sat at the dining room table and drew up a logo, hooked up an answering machine (yes voice mail wasn't invented yet), and was on his way to a great and emerging company. I remember my dad being in a serious car accident where he was transported by helicopter to the hospital with a broken hip. It appeared as though everything was going to be a challenge. However, he pushed himself to heal and had the ability to move the company to incredible heights. I had always wondered if the company would someday be mine to lead and was excited at the thought of learning the business side by side with my dad.

After carefully weighing the decision to leave my bank position, I joined my dad's company as a Sales Manager of a newly formed electronics division. My dad wanted to diversify the company to be a full service security company and not just a security guard company. He knew that the security guard industry was labor intensive and overhead positions such as Human Resource professionals, labor attorneys and similiar needs would eat into profits.

Therefore, we decided to create a diversified full-service security company where we would use technology instead of labor. An example of this was our first entrée into the electronic security business. This business was built on residual income via residential alarm monitoring. From there, we worked our way into the private investigations business. We also created a whole new market of residential alarm customers with our product called the Quick-1. Quick-1 was a Do-It-Yourself alarm system which could be installed by the apartment dweller. This cut the cost for alarm installers. Cameras, access controls, magnetometers, private investigations and security training made us a full service and complete security company. I resigned from the bank and joined the family business with the full intention to be in it for years to come. At the office with my dad, I began to learn about the security industry but more on how to be a leader and entrepreneur. During this time, I was basically a sponge. I learned loads from my dad and about my dad. My dad was, and still is strictly business. I observed him make tough decisions around personnel, contracts and the politics of a business, moving from the small business space to the medium size emerging business space. I learned how similar my dad and I were but I also saw some glaring differences. Differences in priorities, management styles and just the way we operated. We both had a charisma and a work ethic that was uncanny. It was safe to say during this period that I was in awe of my father and really just wanted him to be proud of me. After two years with my dad, he decided to sell his company and encouraged me to start my own security company. Dad provided the initial seed money to launch AREAWIDE Electronic Security Systems, Inc. His company was called AREAWIDE Services Limited and was known all over the Washington Metropolitan area as a leader in security services. In early July 1997, my company won its first government contract for $1.6M to provide security guard services for the General Services Administration at the Voice of America Building in Washington DC. Because the security industry is a 24/7 business, my days were long. I had never worked this hard in my life. To keep costs down, I did all the administrative work. The business development was also on my to-do list and yes…I kept a security guard uniform in my car just in case…just like my dad did. Our first contract didn't mean we were rich at all.

Most small companies get contracts in this industry and depending on the size of the contract, we would average somewhere between 1/2 % to 12% profit which isn't much when you include insurance, fleet vehicles, office rent, overhead, etc. Yes, the days were very long indeed…in the morning I would sit in the office alone as there was no staff and do paperwork. In the afternoon, I would conduct meetings to try to drum up business. In the evening, I would do both: conduct meetings and paperwork. At night, I would don a security guard uniform and sit on a security post with another guard. Sometimes in a school, sometimes in a hotel, wherever security was needed, I was there. I remember one night being in an empty construction site with no light. I will never forget the chill as the night air turned to morning. The sounds made by the animals all around me. The bathroom…wait there wasn't a bathroom. This was the way I lived for the first year of the company's existence. I would sit at a post everywhere I could which was good as I could see how it feels to be a security guard. I sat in freezing cold buildings. I sat in buildings with rats. Like all security guards, I wanted to shut my eyes and go to sleep but I'm proud to say I always kept my eyes wide open.

Then the company started to grow quickly with contracts coming in left and right. We were winning contracts and providing great service. In my late 20s with millions flowing through the business account, I became arrogant. I was immature and couldn't really appreciate the blessings that had been bestowed on me. Even though I paid myself less than $50K/year, I was still so immature and so arrogant but I couldn't see it. I do believe that it takes a certain level of arrogance to lead people, however mine was over the top. I can remember thinking I could do everything and had no value for others' opinions and I was a horrible listener. My way of listening was "you listen to me."

In 2001, the company hit a major crossroads. September 11, 2001 (another day where everyone in America can tell you where they were) started for me as a day at the Marriott in Greenbelt MD for a networking breakfast. After the breakfast, I was driving down the beltway and noticed smoke just over the Woodrow Wilson Bridge in Virginia. I also noticed the office had been trying to reach me several times. When I called the office, I was

informed that terrorists had attacked the Pentagon. Being
in the security guard business, protecting government
buildings was a busy day for our team. Our company grew
to $15M that day. Whew...I can remember not sleeping
for days afterward. From doing interviews on television
and magazines, literally transporting weapons, food and
paychecks to employees as they hunkered down at their
posts, this 24-hour span was a complete blur. During my
company's growth, I decided to do something against the
grain and become a union ally. As a strategy, my dad and
I discussed increasing the guards' wages and unions could
help us do that. Well, this was the beginning of the end
as the unions did get the wages up but the newly formed
Homeland Security department wasn't quick to sign off
on the increased wages. During the days after the 9/11
terrorists attacks, the Bush Administration decided to create
a department to protect our Homeland. This caused major
turmoil around our contracts. Our contracts were originally
with the General Services Administration (GSA). GSA is
the "property manager" for Federal Government buildings.
Security, janitorial services, landscaping, etc were part
of the GSA's responsibilities. Still today, the GSA is

responsible for government buildings except for security services. These contracts were transferred to Homeland Security which meant trouble for my company. True to our word, we paid the employees increased wages while waiting for Homeland Security to reimburse the increased wages. It never happened. My dad and I were in major disagreement on how this would be handled. I wanted to sue the government and walk off post. As a loyal veteran, my dad disagreed. He felt like we should stay in this time of turmoil and support our Federal Government. We also weren't being paid for our additional work assigned due to the September 11 terrorists attacks. On 9/11, my company was invoicing Homeland Security about $1.2M per month for security services. Unfortunately, Homeland was paying the invoicing for the Temporary Additional Services (TAS). TAS was the work that was attached to existing contracts. Over a period of two years, Homeland Security ran up a bill of $1.2M that was at times being over 90 days past due on our regular invoices which totaled $1.2 per month. Sadly, we offered a ½% discount in writing to Homeland if they paid in a net 10-day term. They never used the net 10 days and in some cases, the clock is still ticking.

Finally, I started to mature. I started to listen. I listened to my dad and did both...I sent a letter to my Congressman requesting assistance in regards to the severely tardy outstanding invoices owed from the government while continuing to stay on post. We did win an award for outstanding service from the Bush Administration and were still growing leaps and bounds, however the pressure to make payroll every week was wearing on me. Our payroll was $500K every other Friday. There were mornings I would come into the office and turn on my computer only to see the company in the negative $800K. Paychecks were to be handed out in just a matter of hours and I didn't have the money. The weight of 500 families was on my shoulders. On September 17, 2003 with the government now owing me $1.27M, I received a fax at 4p. The fax was informing me that the Contracting Officer decided it was easier to find another contractor than to figure out payment to my company. I was numb after reading this. I knew that my life would change forever. As I sat in my office and contemplated what the next day, our last day in business, would look like, I felt every emotion. I was angry. I walked through the office all alone and slammed pictures from the wall. I talked to myself asking myself why? I cried. I sobbed like a baby knowing that I had failed. Even now, some 13 years later, I get that sick feeling in my stomach. If you ever had butterflies from anxiety, imagine an elephant stomping on the inside of your stomach. This is what I felt like…life…my life would never ever be the same. While the fax did explain I would be paid for back invoices "at some point", the options on my contract years would not be renewed.

How did I lose $15M? Let me break it down for you…the company prior to 9/11 had secured about $5M in revenue in it's first couple of years. After 9/11, our client the General Services Administration added so much security we couldn't keep up. Talk about growth…whew!

We were now at 500 employees. 500 employees? I remember when it was just me. Every two weeks I had to make a payroll of $500K so the company itself really only profited about $200K/month. Now you say hmmm that sounds like a lot of money but really it's not.

Without getting too far in the weeds, the easy math is this. That $200K if multiplied by let's say 48 months which is what I had left on my 5 year contract totals about

$9.6M. Now, since the company wasn't being paid the full amount of it's invoices or payments were severely delayed the creditors started to pile up to the tune of about $2M. Add in the already $1.27M which is what we sued the Government for and some other loans etc and there you have it...I'm out $15M.

I still say I'm richer now than I've ever been.

The next day, I showed up at work and hung a sign on our glass doors that the company was closed. Chaos broke out! My phone was blowing up with angry employees wanting to be paid their last paychecks. Vendors and creditor's lawyers were calling me, sending certified mail attempting to collect money. The worst was when I thought I was being followed by some angry employee and I pulled into a police barrack parking lot for safety. I had to arm myself as the death threats were becoming more and more frequent. We had a large office suite and after six years of service, someone had to empty the office in order to avoid paying the rent which was already late.

Piece by piece, I moved every inch of the 10,000 square foot space. It took me about two weeks to put everything in storage and in my garage. I decided to put the company in Chapter 11 bankruptcy to get some breathing room, however even that is expensive. I couldn't file for unemployment as I was an officer of the corporation. After two years in bankruptcy court and hiring a government contract attorney who I couldn't afford, I decided to hire a civil rights attorney. I decided on this strategy as I can remember once in a meeting when I was attempting to collect money owed to the company by the government, an official said in his slowest southern drawl, "hey aren't you Mac's boy?" Mac was a nickname my dad went by and this same individual while coming out of the bathroom dropped a pack of matches on the floor. I saw the matchbox. It had KKK slogans on it. I also wanted a civil rights attorney because I was a small minority business with 95% of its employees being minority. Finally, my reason for hiring a civil rights attorney was all my contracts were sourced for minority owned businesses. I had a press conference with an attorney who is still in practice by the way. I felt great about our case. He put the case in U.S. District Court. I explained this is my last $10K. I need your best effort here. Well, I never heard from him again. This fellow, who is a black man, took my last dollar and ran with it. To add insult to injury, I recently visited his Facebook page and noticed he has information about my case on his page, even though he did next to nothing. Not a day goes by that I'm not reminded of that horrible ending to what was my dream job. Several years later, the local media came to my house and did a story on my company. The question that I'm always asked is, "why didn't Homeland Security pay you?" I give the answer they gave me in 2001. "We are under a national tragedy and for you to ask for your money now is un-American…we will get to it when we can." As the years passed, I would meet lawyers interested in the case who would take a look.

Finally, a lawyer who I really just met in passing said to me…"young man…the government is off the hook for the money after six years." He gave me the policy which is buried in a book called the FAR which is the government's version of a rulebook. And so it was…I will never be paid the $1.27M that's owed. The debt, the shame, the pain will stay with me as long as I allow it to. The end of my company also had negative effects on my family. My marriage ended shortly thereafter. My relationship with my dad was strained. I remember being at a company

Christmas party once and someone at the party mentioned that it was my dad who was jealous of my success and trying to put me out of business. Ridiculous! My dad took a financial hit over this whole transaction. More importantly, it took us years to repair our relationship.

However, I was at a church service in Alabama and the pastor talked about forgiveness. This sermon really resonated with me. I decided to write down the names of people who had hurt me along the way, or people who I just flat out needed to forgive. On that day, I forgave my dad. Although friends who I thought were friends weren't and disappeared, I stayed true to having a forgiving spirit. Things started turning around for me once I started to forgive. For years, people have advised me time and time again, "you should write a book." Well for all those people, it took me a while but here you are. Now, I speak all over the country about this chapter of my life and I even consult with other small business owners to avoid this happening to them. Unfortunately, I spent the six months after losing the company in a deep depression over losing the company. Later, I will detail the exhausting and sometimes improbable road to recovery.

- **SOAK UP EXPERIENCES LIKE A SPONGE.**

So much is placed on traditional education…you know the type, with the formal classroom training. What about the untraditional learning or "experiences"? Believe me…I have learned so much more outside the classroom than inside. I use just a few things to really help me learn. I listen to those who are wiser than me. That would be anyone a day older than I am. They have been on the planet longer therefore know a day more than I do. I listen to those who have more experience in something specific than I have for that same topic, no matter their age. I listen to people who have selected faith as their life's work. They talk to God so I know they have some experiences I could learn from them. Notice I continued to say I listen. I also practice. I practice to see what works for me and how I can apply it into habit. Practice truly does make perfect. There is nothing like experience. I've learned that in coaching and just in life in general. The best way to experience is to just do it. Nike said it best. It wouldn't be an experience if you don't do it. Experience first, learn second, grow third…but do it.

• YOU COULD BE HERE TODAY AND GONE TOMORROW.

Sounds a little morbid I know but it gets your attention. It's a call for urgency. This Extra Point is a procrastinator's nightmare. Nobody wants to talk about the "d-word" but with all that goes on in the world today you must think about it (death). I encourage you to live life to its fullest for tomorrow truly isn't promised. Work hard and take time to smell the roses. Make sure your last conversations with people are positive and not negative. Leave your mark on this world. Talk to God and before you know it today is gone and tomorrow is here and you get to do it all over again.

• LIFE ISN'T FAIR ESPECIALLY WITH CORPORATE GREED IN THE AIR.

The Extra Point here is basically money changes the way people think. I have seen money take the kindest person and turn them into the meanest. The workplace is a haven for this "Extra Point." I have seen so many times good employees and employers totally change their character and core values because of the old mighty dollar.

Chapter Six

"Focus on the Team"

I had just come off the most difficult loss in my life; losing my company. I had decided to finally leave my bedroom after staying in it for about five months, due to a very deep depression. From September 18, 2003 to Feb 2, 2004, depression had totally taken over my life. I would wake up but had no energy to get up. I would lie in bed for hours. Not really sleep, just lying there. First on my back then on my stomach. I tossed and turned all day. Sunlight coming through the window was like kryptonite for me. For some strange reason, at 6pm, I would get up and turn on the television. I would watch a show called the Parkers. The Parkers starred comedian Monique and it was a really silly show. It did make me laugh a little…then I would watch my favorite soap opera, "The Guiding Light." The Guiding Light was special to me because when I was a kid and my mom was pregnant with my sister Kathy, I would run home and watch it with her. Watching it as an adult reminded me of those formative years. After the Parkers and a taped version of the soap opera, I would shower and eat some very light dinner then go back to sleep. I lived this way until one day, I decided to wake up and get up and sign onto the computer.

I hadn't turned on a computer in months. The first thing I did was google Mike Gottfried. I noticed Coach Gottfried was in Mobile, Alabama and was leading a regional non-profit called Team Focus. Team Focus is a mentoring organization which ran leadership camps for young men without fathers. I was in my first year at Crossland (as Head Football Coach) and had seen the effects of growing up without a father firsthand with some of my players. I emailed Coach Gottfried and hoped to hear something back. I had sent him many letters right after his termination at PITT but never received a reply. During the summer of 2004, while coaching a football camp at PITT, I received a call from Coach Gottfried. "Keith! It's Mike!" I was so happy. Ironically, I was at PITT and Coach was in DC lobbying Capitol Hill for funding for Team Focus. He asked me what I was up to and I said "nothing, I just lost

$15M." Coach Gottfried invited me to a camp in Dallas, Texas. I remember being excited but wasn't quite sure where this was going to lead. Once I arrived in Dallas, I immediately was struck by how gentle Coach Gottfried was with these kids. It was a side of him I hadn't seen. Coach Gottfried then asked me to speak to the kids who were participating in a leadership camp as part of Team Focus. I wasn't a professional speaker or anything but he told me I had a gift and a story to tell. "Keith, tell them about what you have been through" he encouraged. So I spoke, again and again with the Bible and God as the support. Had I tapped into something? Was this my real calling? I guess Coach Gottfried saw what I saw because the next thing I knew Coach Gottfried offered me a full-time job as a leader at Team Focus. This was one of the best experiences of my life. I learned so much from these young men, who were growing up without a dad in their lives. I was stepping into the shoes of the father figure. Night after night, ball games, dinners, music recitals, back to school nights, etc. The blessings were pouring out from Columbus, Ohio to San Diego, California to Las Vegas, Nevada to Ann Arbor, Michigan. Every four days I'm in a new town motivating, leading and developing these young men. Who would have known that this was the best therapy for me? The road to recovery was right in my face. I'm a coach! This is who I am and I have a few gifts to channel in the direction of those who need support.

To my surprise and honor, in 2006, I reached a real highlight in my life. I was asked to speak on a panel with the First Lady, Laura Bush. Mrs. Bush was a champion for young people and had an initiative called Helping America's Youth. I can remember the Secret Service swooping into Mobile days prior to her visit. I remember finally meeting her and we (unplanned) had on the same color jackets. In a quiet moment, Mrs. Bush said "Keith, you say you are from DC? Her Texas accent was still noticeable. I said "yes I am. I was born and raised in the Capitol of the Free World." After our panel discussion, the First Lady actually shed a tear based on my commentary about mentoring young men without fathers in their lives." She leaned over and said "Keith...I will see you back in DC." I can still here it today.) Through this initiative, Team Focus was receiving national attention.

Coach Gottfried was still on ESPN and I was still

coaching at Crossland, however Team Focus was growing leaps and bounds. I was in the "soul saving" business. My faith had grown so much stronger. How could it not? I was witness to so many blessings right before my very eyes. I saw young men commit to Christ and stay off drugs. I met so many young men who I still keep in touch with today. I can remember sitting with them on park benches and just talking. We would talk about life and all the different twists and turns and how to navigate through them. (So many stories…I remember a young man hiding under his bed because he didn't want to leave camp and go back home where there was no father and I literally crawled under the bed with him to talk him out.) While every young man I met had a story, it was Andre Taylor's story that was most compelling. I met Andre when he was in the 8th grade. His aunt brought him to me and informed me he would be attending Crossland High School in the fall. Andre was an amazing athlete who I had to coach into being a quarterback. He had it all: great looks, charisma, and athleticism. He also had a chip on his shoulder because he was growing up without a father. During his freshman year, Andre wanted to be the starting quarterback and probably could have been, however he needed to stay on the Junior Varsity and grow. In the fall, Andre was a student-athlete. In the summer, he was a member of Team Focus. Like me, Andre would fly all over the country meeting new friends who were just like him. In his sophomore season, while becoming the starting quarterback, he was also starting to cut up in class. Andre wasn't the best student. I had to constantly stay on him about his school work. I remember his Math teacher, Tim Washington yes…the same guy I call "Wash" earlier in the book, inform me that Andre was skipping his class. I ran Andre for hours and he just wouldn't tire. I had to discipline him a different way. Junior year approaches and college recruiters like Andre on the field but off the field, the grades and sometimes misbehaviors in school were a turn off to college recruiters. I explained to Coach Gottfried that we need to change Andre's brand to get him college marketable. Coach Gottfried made a call to Jim Farmer. Jim was a retired executive with GMAC. GMAC was a major sponsor for Team Focus via the GMAC Bowl played in Mobile, Alabama. Coach Gottfried explained that Andre was going from house to house with no known address and Andre needs to change. Coach Gottfried asked Jim for some clothes for Andre. Andre reluctantly accepted the clothes and the change began to happen. Andre started going to class and his anger was (became versus was) manageable. Andre even told his story to Laura Bush, and when she entered the room, it was Andre who pulled her chair out for her. Wow…this kid had come a long way. With senior year upon us, Andre and I both knew we had a veteran team and it was our time to win and win big, and bring Crossland High School back to prominence. We started the season with a victory. Around mid-season, Andre and another captain of the team and Team Focus member Robert Allen got into a fight in practice. (I can recall the local newspaper and parents questioning my decision.) At this time, and against the wishes of everyone, I benched Andre and then moved him to Wide Receiver. I knew what I was doing. On the field, he was a better receiver than quarterback and had a chance at college football as a receiver. Off the field, he needed to grow up and be humble and learn that there are consequences for bad behavior. After the season ended, sadly, college coaches weren't feeling Andre's grades.

Again, I reached out to Coach Gottfried for help. He contacted a junior college in Mississippi and asked the coach to review Andre's highlight tape and allow him to come for a visit. Andre and I flew to Huntsville, Alabama and then drove to the middle of nowhere Mississippi. While in the rental car, Andre told me all about his life and how this was a trip that would map out his future. I elected to talk to Andre about the long and winding road we were traveling, and how our ancestors were probably treated unfairly on the very roads during slavery and even now. A great bonding session came to an end when we pulled up at Northeast Mississippi Junior College. As we walked to the coaches' office and he sat with Andre, I didn't know what to think. Andre was excited. Finally, after numerous meetings, the coach said "Andre, welcome to Northeast Mississippi." Andre and I went for lunch. As we were walking, we saw a pickup truck with several white males in the back of the truck. Their welcome to Mississippi was a little different as they yelled "hey nigga, hey nigga." We both were shocked. It didn't put a damper on the day though…we had lunch and went back to the hotel. I was exhausted and told Andre I was going to run to Wal-Mart and pick up a few things and then come back for a nap. About an hour later, I arrived back at the hotel and Andre was just sitting and staring at the walls. He had been crying. I said "Andre, what have you been doing?" He said "Coach Howard...I called every family I ever stayed with and told them I'm going to college." I couldn't help but cry. This kid had written down a list of people who had helped him along the way. Andre ended up playing college football for two years. Eventually, he came back to DC once his mom passed away. I was at the funeral and just watching his strength was amazing to see. To know I had been a part of his growth was so rewarding. About ten years from the day Andre and I went to Mississippi, I received a call. The caller ID said DC Department of Corrections. I was afraid to answer as usually that means someone is in jail. I answered the phone and I hear "Sup Coach!" Andre? I was like, oh no what's next...well what was next was great. Andre was working as a corrections officer in the DC jail and wanted to catch up, and when I told him I was working for a bank, he said "good, you can help me figure out my retirement plan." Even today, Andre and I still keep in touch with phone calls two or three times per year.

Unfortunately, my time at Team Focus ended after a six year run but with a lifetime of memories. Our funding dried up and the organization had to downsize. The DC area was Team Focus' most expensive region. I thought about moving to Mobile, Alabama but after being in DC all my life, DC is where I wanted to be. DC is where I was born and it is home for me.

Once again, I was out of a job. During the worst economic downfall in our country's history, I'm out here interviewing. I figured out quickly that I never really had to look for a job. My interviewing skills were awful. My resume needed a major overhaul. Finally, I interviewed for a job at a bank as a manager. I got the job but my heart was never really in it. Retail banking is a tough job. The first two years opened my eyes to a world I had only heard of but never really knew, and that was corporate America. Corporate greed, racism, reverse racism, the haves and have not's, I learned it all. My last two years really told that story as I lost my job. I was treated unfairly by the management and like when I lost my security company, I had an opponent who was too big to compete against.

One thing I did learn from both Team Focus, the bank, my security company etc…it's all about the team. Every coach I've had and every player I've coached has preached that it's really all about the team. During my many travels with Team Focus, part of our curriculum was being a good teammate. Focus, part of our curriculum was being a good teammate. Focus on the team, no matter how big or how small, no matter the task, no matter what...focus on the team and the team will win.

THE

★ EXTRA POINTS ★

- **CREATING, BUILDING AND NURTURING RELATIONSHIPS ARE IMPORTANT WHILE CONNECTING THE DOTS OF LIFE.**

The extra point here is just a reminder to go the extra mile for your relationships. Whether it's a spouse, family, friend, co-worker, teammate, etc. make sure you are constantly creating new relationships and nurturing the existing relationships. Why have I found this extra point so essential to winning? Like anything else in life, if it's is worth anything you will probably need support and assistance along the way. In order to connect the dots of life, it will take an entire team of supporters to do so. In order for those supporters to be there when you need them, you must be a reliable and dependable spouse, friend, etc to them. In an age of social media, cell phones and other ways to stay connected there really isn't an excuse to take an extra minute to go that extra mile for a friend. The blessings for the stewardship of a friendship will come back to you thousands of times over.

- **DON'T BLOCK GOD'S BLESSINGS.**

During my tenure at Team Focus, I learned so much about

God and what God tries to teach all of us. Since Team Focus was ministry work, we always had pastors visit to chat with our campers about God, faith and the Bible. During one of the sermons, I took these notes which I have carried for years. I learned a very easy "Extra Point." Don't block God's blessing. It is so simple to block the blessings God has in store for you. As I list these three blessing blockers, see if any pertain to you. At some point in my life, each one has affected me. Negativity is the first blessing blocker I wrote. Being negative or even speaking in negative connotations are blessing blockers. I work really hard to make sure that when I speak it's always in the positive even if it means I may need to say more words to avoid the negative ones.

The next blessing blocker is the past. The past is exactly that the past. This one was a struggle for me to overcome. I have a few bumps in my past that make it difficult to forgive and to move forward. The technique I use to move forward from the past is to quickly think about the positives of that negative. For example, whenever I hear of a football team going winless in a season, I think about my first season as a Head Coach at Crossland High School. Once that pain of past losses creeps in my brain, I immediately channel the positives that came from those losses like the lasting relationships made during those losses. I met some great players and coaches during that tough time and chose to spend my thoughts on calling them and reconnecting, asking how they are doing and thanking them for going through those times with me.

The next blessing blocker is fear. Fear is the devil's favorite thing. This one also has become my most difficult to overcome. When I find myself fearful, I have nothing but prayer to help me. There have been times when I have been afraid of failure of a project. I prayed on this fear and within moments I'm able to overcome.

- **BE A GOOD TEAMMATE.**

It is so important to be a good teammate. Whether you are on a sports team or just in a family unit, being a good teammate works. Whenever I have transitioned teams, I have always started with being a good teammate. If you can get a team to think this way it will win. Imagine your teammate saying to you "hey what can I do to help you?" How does that make you feel? When you know your teammate cares about you it makes you want to work a little harder for them. The military is probably the best example I have seen of the good teammate. An oath is taken to protect our Country however in the military they readily jump in front of bullets and suicide bombers to be good teammates.

Chapter Seven

"A Win in a Loss"

Most of this book has been about my travels, experiences and life lessons both on the field and off. However, this chapter is different. This chapter is very personal too me. Let me explain the two reasons I chose to write this chapter…First, I am glad to be alive and able to share these life lessons and these Extra Points. Life is so precious. There were days in my life when I wasn't sure I would ever write a book, go for a walk, get out of bed or even see the next moment. The second reason is to bring awareness to mental health issues, especially in black males. For me, I believe mental health could decay as early as your childhood. In my case, I believe I had a wonderful childhood, however, over the years there were experiences that surely weakened my own mental health. Nothing upset me more than September 17, 2003, the day I lost my company. The cost of this incident and its by-products dragged me into a deep depression. By-products like unemployment, failed relationships, financial ruin and overwhelming stress were agonizing. During this painful time, I also suffered more repercussions like strained finances, bad health like high blood pressure, weight gain and severe sinus problems. Further complications included a devastating loss of family, a strained relationship with my dad and then my own nuclear family became splintered. These pain points are hard to write even now a decade later. Ironically, it wasn't these life moments which would bring me to my knees. In 2012, I finally landed on my feet. I had steady income. I had a nice place to stay overlooking FedEx Field. Everything was good…I'd even mended fences with my dad and had a regular schedule to spend time with my two daughters. I had new suits for work, I was working in downtown DC, meeting new people, still coaching football and having tremendous success. Things were turning around slowly.

Surpisingly, it was moving forward that actually set me back, like a penalty flag in a football game. Let me tell you the story…I met some really great people. Initially, I met great listeners, some with great intentions, some without. I would share my life story and how difficult it had been. Some would encourage me to have faith, some encouraged me to push. It was during this period that a friend suggested that I go to professional counseling. I was like, "who me?" I'm Coach Howard, I'm fine... I don't need counseling. For the first time, there was a person who didn't fear telling me what I needed to hear, not what I wanted to hear. A person who cared enough to let me know I was a good person who needed to address his anxiety, patience, possible depression and narcissism. As I attempted to progress and move to my next phase of life, I guess I just couldn't until I addressed those mental health issues. In fact, I was suffering from depression. Instead of being able to move on with my life, I was stuck in negativity, like a dark cloud. Stuck in the past of losing my company, which I felt had led to the separation with my loved ones. In an effort to move on, I made the decision to pursue happiness at a different address. Simply put, I moved out, and then moved into a new place with new roommates. I'll keep it simple...that same friend who cared enough to tell me I needed some counseling once again stood up to me and told me what I needed to hear and did what I didn't want them to do. We had a disagreement.

I was wrong. Said some terrible things, made horrible accusatory comments to that friend and finally on February 2, after many trials and tribulations, they left. I was angry at first. What in the world was I thinking? What was I doing? I can remember being at football practice waiting, standing in the elements, but realized that "happiness" was no longer there. I finally realized I needed to move on and that friend wasn't coming back. After numerous texts and emails, I realized the game was over. Time had expired.

Bitten by the flu bug that week, I even missed work. I was in complete co-dependency. What about the bills? What about the companionship? What about our plans for the weekend!? I was so used to "happiness" or what I thought was "happiness" that I was lost. Later that week, I went to church. It was during that service that I made up my mind that I had to change. If I was just given the chance, I would change for the better. I remember how suddenly I had no texts, no calls, no emails no nothing – for weeks! Everything was still, everything was quiet, and I had time to reflect on my own happiness, depending only on myself. I guess the universe was listening.

I decided to begin my change with a couple of different

items. First, talk to my family and finally grieve past losses. The conversations were amazing, just sitting, listening and always supporting. Next, I decided to speak to my mom about how I needed her help to get through this pain and it would be a journey. I explained to her that I needed her to spend more time with my two girls and help me to make this transition seamless. Then I started to exercise to try to take care of me. I changed my eating habits and decided to even bring together my daughters and my new friends.

I knew I was improving and addressing my issues. I got some counseling from a work referral once a week and that was helping too.

Things started to get tougher however. So, I decided to increase the number of hours of counseling to include pastoral upport. Many were encouraging me to rely more on my family for help. They said to stay in faith. But one day, I was on my way to football practice when my world crumbled again. The pressure of the inconsistent and lack of support in personal relationships had finally taken its toll at the most unexpected moment. I was distraught. Everything began to spiral out of control. I began losing weight. Did I ever lose weight? From February 2 to May 1, I lost 42 pounds. I grieved through the days, and at work, my head was in a fog. I had no idea that things were going to get even worse. Swallowing the pill of being co-dependent on one person albeit a good person and a person who cared enough to walk away it still was agonizing.

After 20 years of coaching, I'd never missed a game, however I did miss one because of my health. So on April 12th, I returned to the field. I was coaching my second women's tackle football team. Visibly shaken, weak and battered, the players and my coaching staff could tell something was very wrong. After losing a nail biter and walking off the field, my dear friend, Coach Wash asked if I was ok. I'll come stay with you, he said, something is really wrong. I went home and the depression overwhelmed me. Wash continued to call me, but I wouldn't answer. I was going to do the unthinkable. I had trouble sleeping so my doctor had prescribed some sleeping pills. I looked at the pills in the cabinet long and hard and decided to put four in my mouth. Fortunately for me, I had a very close friend (Joy) that prevented it from happening. While sitting in my bedroom with pills in mouth I heard some noise outside my window. Joy was a former player who used to be a roommate of mine as well. She sensed at the game that something was really wrong and took a cab over when I didn't answer the phone. She remembered where I kept the spare key and dashed upstairs to talk me off the cliff. Immediately after that, I got some medical help and was put on 24-hour watch. I had intense therapy. Due to the severity of my issues, again I attended clinical and pastoral counseling as well as psychiatric. I completed hours and hours of therapy taking me all the way from birth to current time. Intense admissions and brutal honesty with myself was the best medicine. My diet and an exercise plan was part of my healing. I had daily homework from my entire therapy team. My job offered me short term disability to help me with my healing. In May, after my initial month of therapy, I decided to move out of my townhome in Maryland and live in DC. I found a really cool place in a great neighborhood where I could walk and think. Later that month, my oldest daughter was graduating and I was happy. Even though things were rocky personally, I'd adjusted well with the new counseling and was able to push through it.

In June, I gained back some strength. I gained a few pounds. I went back to work. I started working out again. Walking was a big deal for me. I started a few guilty pleasures like reading, writing, and watching Dateline and the Bold and the Beautiful daily. Finally, on Father's Day with my family, I had defeated depression! That was a great day! I had them all over my house and made a big lunch for everyone. I wore a shirt which read "LIVESTRONG."

Through this time frame, there were so many friends who came to my aid. There was Coach Wash who called all the time to check on me. When I called him, he answered. There was the roommate, (Joy) who took the pills from me and saved me that dark Sunday morning on April 12. Full of joy, she stayed by me throughout that summer and sort of nursed me back to life with walks and long conversations. I've coached hundreds of players but to have a player actually save your life? Now that's something I never thought would happen. I never thought a player would see me that weak. This player pushed me to live and told me every day how much I have to live for and encouraged me to reach my full potential. The odd thing about this was that's what I do. That's what Coach Howard has done so many times. This time, the player was coaching the coach. There were too many friends to list, but I thank them all. How many friends would be there for you as you grieve over what appeared to be a broken heart? People would call with prayers and when you can get others to pray for you, unlikely people, that is a major thing. Thanks to everyone who listened and cared...special thanks to the people I named here.

Mental health in black men is almost a taboo subject. According to Mental Health America, clinical depression is not just "having the blues." Clinical depression is not a weakness but a serious medical illness. Clinical depression can be treated. There are many barriers to defeating depression such as denial, shame, lack of money and even the hopelessness itself. Studies all over the internet show the reasons why black men specifically struggle with depression: from our roots as slaves to exclusion from health care, education, employment, housing etc to our overall socio-economics. Our socio-economic status is clearly linked to such by-products as imprisonment, drug abuse, homelessness etc which increase the risk for poor mental health. How many of you reading this book have had your mental health evaluated? I would encourage you to do just that. We as coaches tell our players to stay healthy, we must also make sure they stay mentally healthy as well. We take our cars for tune ups, we go to the doctor for medical check-ups, we even run our computers through a virus scan so why not check our mental health? While not all of us have access to a mental health professional, we all have access to faith. Praying is free. Counseling helped. In some cases, medication helped. Exercise helped. Changes in my diet helped but nothing defeated depression like prayer. I pray every day. Some days I pray multiple times a day. Jeremiah 29:11 is my favorite prayer and while I have many others, that one is my go to. What's your go to prayer? If you don't know, that's fine, it's never too late to find one. Part of my healing is this book and traveling around the country to share the life of my story. Everybody has a story, however, not every story has a life. My story has a life that is prosperous, not harmful and a life full of hope for a wonderful future.

* IF YOU CAN PICK UP THE PHONE DO SO, YOU JUST MAY SAVE A LIFE.

The Extra Point sounds simple, HOWEVER, how many times have you thought about calling an old friend and then for no apparent reason procrastinated the call to another time? Or how about when you looked at your cell phone and saw an old friend call and you just put them into voicemail with the intent to call them "later?" Well, as much as technology makes life more convenient, perhaps just some "old school" pick up the phone and reach out and touch someone could actually save a life.

* WALKING IS GREAT FOR YOUR MENTAL HEALTH.

It's true. I'm living proof. When I moved from the MD suburbs to urban DC, I began to walk. Walking releases endorphins and makes me sleep better. I just feel fitter and more confident. Walking and seeing the trees and hearing the sounds just decreases the stress and less stress equals more happiness.

* PRAYING IS FREE.

Ever heard the phrase, "nothing in life is free?" Well

I found something that not only is free but its value is priceless. Can you imagine paying nothing for something so valuable? I didn't always use this valuable chat with God. Life will bring those of us crazy enough not to use prayer to talk to God to be regular visitors with God. When I pray to God, it's like a conversation with a friend, a father, a mentor. The real greatness of our God is when he speaks back to me. God guides HIS children for free. There is no cost for prayer. Buy it! It works every time and all the time. Invest in it! It is recession proof and never ceases to amaze and astound.

- **IT'S NOT WHAT YOU SAY BUT HOW YOU SAY IT.**

Words can be very painful. Coaching as long as I have I known this to be true. Sometimes as a coach, I've had to tell a player that there performance isn't quite up to par. There are many ways to say this. Coach: You just are having a tough time today reading defenses. I'm going to go with the backup quarterback. Or you could say...you stink and are clueless get on the bench. As you can see the first way was easier to receive versus the second statement. Be careful how you say what you say. Talk to people the way you would want to be spoken too. The extra point here is try to speak without negative words and watch your tone and inflection.

Chapter Eight

"You're the Inspiration"

When I initially thought about writing this book, I
was afraid. Afraid of what, you might ask? I was afraid of
failure. I've never really been afraid of failure until I lost
my company. When it comes to going for it, I have pretty
much always done that. When I'm on the sideline, I'm an
aggressive play caller, and when I'm in the boardroom,
I'm not afraid to say what others are thinking. But writing
a book...that was new territory. I needed inspiration.
There were two things that I knew would inspire me and
ensure that the fear bug wouldn't raise its ugly head. First,
developing people, helping people, encouraging others is
who I am and the intent of the book is just that! Next...
this one is so very easy...Kennedy and Fallon Howard, my
daughters.

Now, before I demonstrate how these two very special
individuals actually inspire me, let me say that there is
no playbook to parenting. Thanks so much to Felecia.

Kennedy and Fallon couldn't ask for a better mom. A pat on the back, kudos and praise aren't enough to describe the job she has done with Kennedy and Fallon.

While I was coaching someone else's child, she was coaching our kids. Yes, co-parenting is a new wrinkle for us but we have accomplished that masterfully. See the rest of the chapter as evidence.

Now world...I introduce to you my inspiration... Kennedy and Fallon Howard!

My daughters are my life's inspiration. Every parent says their children inspire them but I want to do more than say it. I want to express it for the world to hear. The beauty of having two girls three years apart is that there's enough room in my heart to make room for their differences. Kennedy Howard is an absolute delight. Kennedy, aka Daddy's girl, aka Keith Jr. was born on the same date in November that John F. Kennedy was assassinated. The nurse said ,"oh did you name your daughter that because of the former President?" I didn't even know that she was born on the same date. Kennedy was born with jaundice and a really bad case of it. She came home on Thanksgiving Day only to return a few days later. It was so painful to watch her get her bilirubin (which is a needle in the heel) checked every few hours. I used to sit beside her incubator and watch her inch around the incubator. She had her eyes blindfolded because of the strong light. Kennedy recovered from the jaundice and came home. I had no idea what lack of sleep was until she came home. We've all been there right? The baby doesn't sleep. Well this baby really didn't sleep...but I found a way to get her to sleep and that was holding her against my chest and singing Barney the Dinosaur songs. My voice is deep and my chest vibrates when I talk. Kennedy liked that feeling... it soothed her. If I stopped, she woke up...so there were nights when I would sleep standing up and humming that song "I love you" from the Barney the Dinosaur show. In kindergarten, I noticed Kennedy was having a tough time adapting socially to being in all day kindergarten.

Mom and I decided to put her in daycare to let her get used to the whole separation anxiety thing. Again, this strong willed young kid would fight, scratch and claw so that mom and I wouldn't go to work and leave her at daycare. Thank goodness for Ms. Evelene. She worked at the daycare and was so good with Kennedy. Kennedy met her first and oldest friend at Tall Oaks Early Learning Center, her friend Alexus. They are still friends today and now they go to concerts together to scream for Justin Bieber.

On Kennedy's third birthday, she had to share the lime light with her new baby sister, Fallon, aka Daddy's Princess, aka Keith III. Fallon came at a very difficult time. Just a few months prior to Fallon's birth, Felecia's mom passed away. I was very concerned. As expected, Felecia took her mother's passing really hard and I was worried about premature delivery or complications. Instead, mom held steady and out came this enormous baby. Fallon was a huge baby. I can remember being in the delivery room just like I was with Kennedy. The difference with Fallon was we had been there before and so nothing was new except those enormous contractions. It was tough sitting in the room and watching the contractions on the monitor and seeing how much pain Felecia was in. I knew this kid was going to have the same strong will that her older sister had. Like her sister, Fallon attended Tall Oaks for day care and then off to elementary school with her sister. In elementary school, I noticed Kennedy struggling a little in math but other than that, she was all good in her other classes. By the time middle school came around, we decided the girls would attend private school. For the first time, the sisters Howard were in uniform and going to mass. Private school was tough initially. The rigor of the academics and the cost were tough on child and parent. The first school we put them in was also very elite. I had trouble adapting to the snobby attitudes of the parents and the faculty. I pride myself on being "of the people" and I struggled with that atmosphere. After a year, I decided to try the local private school in our community. This was my second time trying to get the girls into this school as the first time we were placed on a waiting list. I begged the principal to please consider us. Note to parents out there. Get in on private schools admission early and often because it is important and it's political. I've seen so many good families passed by and it's sad. Once you get your children in private schools, be visible. It helps to be in the know. I was also concerned for numerous reasons about which direction their academics would lead them. Socially, the girls became involved in Girl Scouts. I'm sure some of you can remember the cookie drives. At one point, I had over

1000 boxes of cookies in my garage. I also was coaching football. I would pick the girls up from school and head straight to football practice. They would be around to get water, help set up cones or just remind daddy that it was time to end practice.

I will never forget the one practice when a player, who needed to toughen up and lose some weight, actually raced Fallon. This player sat in the corner of our football meeting room while we were watching film and kept asking me questions. Basically, his questions were excuses. There one of my speeches was born…"What if You Were Good?" I kept asking questions starting with the words "what if?" Fallon ended up beating him that day in a 40-yard sprint and he was a better player for it. He lost weight, changed his work ethic on the field and off and even got a job. Like I said, Daddy's girls did whatever to help daddy win a football game. As they began to grow up, we started having Kennedy tested for she was struggling to take tests. Kennedy also started to have some anxiety around attending high school. In my community, the public schools were lacking the environment I was looking for and I decided to send Kennedy to a Catholic private high school. Bishop McNamara High School was a safe haven for us. I had coached there for a few seasons and knew most of the staff. There were two things I didn't know about Bishop McNamara. They had a program for students that needed a little more enrichment academically called the St. Joseph's program, and they had an outstanding theatre arts program. Kennedy flourished in both. The tough part was I lost my job with Team Focus when Kennedy was a freshman at Bishop McNamara. Fortunately, with the grace of God, I got a new job just in time for the tuition payment. Fallon, on the other hand, was in her sister's footsteps in middle school. Fallon was flourishing academically and I started to think about having both girls at Bishop McNamara. In Kennedy's freshman year, she ran into a bully! I was shocked. My plan had failed. I was looking for that safe haven and found a bully. Instead however, the administration immediately worked to remedy the situation and Kennedy was fine. Kennedy found her own little niche. She was originally anxious about making friends but did she ever make friends. The theatre was Kennedy's friend. I can still remember how proud I was attending her first high school musical. With her sister in the audience cheering, Kennedy sang and danced her heart out. Then it was Fallon's turn to shine and shine she did. Out the gate, Fallon hit the academics hard. Having Fallon at Bishop McNamara with Kennedy really allowed the two sisters to grow individually. Even though Fallon was called "Kennedy's sister" the first year, Fallon began to make her own niche. Mock trial, yoga club, honor roll and yes theatre. Fallon joined her sister on the stage. Remember how proud you were when you saw your child on stage dancing and singing? Every time I left one of their shows I was in awe. Then it's senior year. Kennedy has so many things going on and it was cool to just sit back and soak it up. I hadn't experienced anything like it. Things had changed since I was a senior. After winning Most Enthusiastic at her theatre arts awards night all four years, graduation was upon us. What a day! Talk about proud…I was beyond proud for academics didn't come easy for Kennedy. Mom had always said Kennedy is having trouble. I always chalked it up to immaturity. Once graduation came and went, it was onto "fangirling." "Fangirling" as Kennedy calls it is when I guess extreme fanatical behavior for a music group. This was Kennedy's favorite past time. She is a social media fiend and loves Justin Bieber, Disney and all that goes with it. After numerous visits to a specialist, it was our turn to celebrate Kennedy's place on the autism spectrum. Since then, I have done tons of reading on autism and am even more amazed at Kennedy's ability to work a room, con daddy out of cash, find her way to meet and greets with pop stars all over the country and just be Kennedy. Meanwhile, it also afforded me the opportunity to watch her sister blossom and celebrate her older sister. Fallon carried on the Howard name at Bishop McNamara with grades as high as 3.9 with an honors schedule, a position as a peer minister and as a member of the National Honor Society!

Currently, after Fallon and I sifted through mail to decide which college she will attend the University of Maryland was decided over my beloved PITT. Kennedy is studying at community college and acquiring her first job at a retail store in the local mall and of course still fangurling. All of us can brag on our kids, however I'd like to share the real inspiration my kids bring to my life. As you read through all the other chapters, I've had some adversity in my life. I've seen some high times and low times. In the lowest of times, it's been a picture of Kennedy and Fallon at five years old and two years old respectively, and another picture of them at seventeen and fourteen. I look at those pictures every single day and I see myself. I see daddy's girl...Kennedy. She has every quality that Keith has. She's quirky very quirky. She listens to all kinds of music, hates to wake up in the morning and is kind to a fault. Then there's daddy's princess...Fallon. The little lawyer, as I call her, has every quality Coach Howard has. Matter of fact, determined as all get out and all about justice for all. As they have grown older now, it's even more evident... not because they both wear glasses like I do, not because they are a little slack in the pants like I used to be (there's still a little slack)...but just because when I look at them, when I listen to them, when I observe them, it's eerily similar to both versions of me. Nothing keeps me going like Kennedy and Fallon. Whether it was sleeping standing up when Kennedy was little or skipping meals to make sure Fallon got the same education Kennedy was getting, even though I didn't have a job. Whether it's rooting for Kennedy as she displays the innocence of a pre-adolescence or advising Fallon when she thinks someone isn't so innocent in their motives...they inspire me! For a guy who has traveled all over this country inspiring audiences of all shapes and sizes, even I need to gain inspiration from somewhere...Kennedy and Fallon, thank you for providing all the inspiration I need. The times when I surely have no ego is when I'm being a dad. The compassion for my children keeps me grounded. On those late nights, when I have come in from a day when I needed to have ego to lead people, it was Kennedy and Fallon whose compassion and admiration was so strong they would say..."hey daddy what did you do today?" They would say it with an innocence that immediately let the air out of my big head. What I've accomplished or owned means nothing when I'm with my girls. It's like I'm just totally humbled. Humbled because I understand that winning truly is humility. I've done some dumb things in my story yet I have learned so much from my two girls. I've learned to be kind over being right. I learned stress really isn't cool and most of all I've learned even the leader and the motivator needs something to motivate them. Kennedy and Fallon Howard do absolutely that for me!

THE

★ EXTRA POINTS ★

• STAY IN TUNE WITH YOUR KIDS AS THEY GROW.

It's so easy to lose contact with your children as they grow. Just take a look at PTA meetings from elementary to middle to high school, and how the attendance dwindles. Now with the advancement of technology, children are so focused on iPhones, social media and hundreds of cable channels that they barely lift their heads up to talk anymore. Coaching has helped me to ensure that I stay in tune with my own children because I've watched so many parents clueless to who their kids are. After games or even practices, I take moments out to talk to players and then when I meet their parents, it's like meeting a total stranger. Use technology to increase your time and attention to your children, not decrease it. When you can couple today's technology with the past traditions before technology, I can guarantee you will be so in tune with your children. Being in tune with your children puts them at an advantage from their peers because so many children are disconnected from the very people who brought them here and they depend on most. My daughters are 21 and 18 years old. Hard years to stay connected but I make sure that if I get a sniff of disconnect, we are going to go to McDonald's and sit down and eat. We are going to watch a television show together. We are going to jump in the car, go for a ride sans the headphones, radio and cell phone. Stay in tune with your children as they grow and make sure of every Extra Point you can give them to soak up, learn from and share it.

• **FATHER/DAUGHTER RELATIONSHIPS ARE IMPORTANT.**

There are thousands of common sense periodicals around the topic of father/daughter relationships and the importance of them. However, all I need to do is think about my relationship with Kennedy and Fallon. It's very simple what my plan was and still is today.

First, my daughters will feel safe as long as I'm breathing. Period. The end.

Second, I will always protect them. My daughters matter and I show them that by telling them and by investing in what they are doing in their lives. Whether it's Kennedy attending a One Direction concert or Fallon selecting an internship, whether it's Fallon wearing an appropriate outfit or Kennedy deciding on whether or not she wants her driver's license. It all matters. My daughter's lives matter.

Third, you want a romantic relationship with my daughter...yes I'm old school so come very, very, very correct. Ungroomed hair, pants sagging, can't articulate a sentence...you will be met with a swift no thanks. Here's why...because I have set the bar high for them. Fourth, I'm their biggest cheerleader! My girls can do anything they set their minds too. Would I be surprised if Kennedy is an executive at Disney someday or on a Broadway stage? Nope! Would I be surprised if Fallon is a Federal judge or owns her law practice? Nope! I cheer for them loudly. Finally, my girls know they are "daddy's girls" and that means something. It means they are an extension of me. They know I'm proud to be their dad. It's my favorite job in the whole world. The Extra Point here is that being a parent is important and being a dad to daughters is a big deal to breaking the cycle that is our young MEN being incarcerated or worse.

Chapter Nine

"The Game Plan for Winning"

So now what? Before I even begin to tackle that question let me first answer how I've even gotten this far in writing this book. I kept telling my story. Everywhere I went, the grocery store, the practice field, on stages, on airplanes or just random conversations with strangers, I continued to tell my story. People who I shared it with would always say "you should write a book." For whatever reason, that wasn't enough to motivate me. You are reading the last chapter of my first book. I've seen a lot and done a lot...but there a few more moments to capture in this life. First, I want to thank all of those who have made an impact in my life. Too many to count...my family both near and far, close and not so close, my friends...old ones, new ones, all my players...boys club, intramural, college, high school, women, semi-pro, all who have worked with me and for me bankers, security guards, coaches...those that have taken care of me...doctors, lawyers, accountants, assistant coaches, etc. Those in my inner circle…the Kim Sumner's, Gina DiPella's and Kara Freeman Lee's of the world thanks so much for the hours, weeks, months, years and decades of friendship, conversations and support. If I missed you, I apologize however you know who you are. The way I say thank you is to give back. I want to give back through Extra Points LLC. I am very determined to have my "Extra Points" to millions of people everywhere. I was never one who could just sit back…I have always pressed the envelope. It burns in me to do the extraordinary. Someone asked me once, "when will you stop coaching?" I couldn't even wrap my brain around that…not coaching? Coaching is my passion both on the field and off. Coaching makes me feel good. Coaching is who I am. Developing people is my purpose. Now telling the life of my story seems effortless. My desire has separated me from the ordinary and writing this book affirms this. It doesn't matter what your passion is please don't ignore it. Make no excuses, don't allow others to manipulate you into something else just be determined. Listen to your determination and follow it.

It's time for your call to action! What are you going

to do next? How are you going to get to the next level?
Where will you go? I want to encourage you to move to
greater heights. THIS IS WHERE THE LIFE OF YOUR
STORY BEGINS. Nothing that has a life comes easy…
you must practice not just daily but moment by moment.
You must prepare not for just today but for life. You must
plan continuously to perfect you masterpiece called life.
This was my goal when I started writing Extra Points.
Encouraging and supporting all those who I can't see.
Through football, I've been able to encourage so many who
I have seen however the real fulfillment the real winning
is Hold onto the major touch points throughout the book.
Select a few "Extra Points" from each chapter. I'd like
to highlight a few major "Extra Points" that are found
throughout the book to provide a "game plan" for winning
in YOUR life.

- The most powerful force in the universe is GOD.
- It's not what you say but how you say it.
- We all have choices sometimes the outcomes are
out of our control.
- Adversity builds character.
- You could be here today and gone tomorrow.

- Don't block God's blessings.

- Praying is FREE.

- Father/daughter relationships are important.

- Love GOD love others.

I wish I could say it was so simple to list a few quotes and everything is complete however YOUR call to action will take so much more than that. The complete game plan starts with YOU. Like I've always told my football players, you must always use every one of your senses to fulfill your destiny. Hear and answer the call to action. Yes! This means YOU. See what you can't see. Yes! Believe in YOU. Feel good when not feeling good. Yes! Enjoy the small wins every time YOU win. Smell a rat when YOU can. Yes! If it smells funky it is funky. Taste the nutrition that is success. Yes! YOU can eat up every "extra point" in this book! Next...build YOUR team, if you need some support in YOUR faith...find it! If you need some support from YOUR family...get it! If you need to tweak YOUR inner circle...do it! Next, self-assess YOUR strengths, weaknesses, opportunities and threats. Make a "happiness" list...tell YOURself what makes YOU happy and of course...make that the end game.

This book is a culmination of a story full of life. From chapter one to the last word in this book, I have finally written a story I have lived and told so many times to so many people in so many places. Extra Points is basically me formalizing just that. One day, I just decided to start telling my story in hopes it could mentor, coach and support others. The rest of my life is totally committed to getting to the heart of the experiences and life lessons with the intent to grow others. My focus is to tell stories that are open, candid and thought provoking. While I continue to coach on the field, off the field I am entering a new arena and that's further developing as many people as I can. It is my intent to use my coaching experiences to inspire others to discover their own journey. Life is a compelling story full of twists and turns and it takes a game plan that is strategic yet flexible and adaptable. I'm really excited about is the art of communicating the old-fashioned way through story telling. Just the thought of public speaking in front of an audience makes some people have thumping hearts from excitement and anticipation. For me however, there's a quiet calm to storytelling. I still remember telling my first story on a stage in front of a live audience. I could hardly believe it seeing people in the audience shed a tear or laugh out loud or write me a note full of gratitude. Seeing these displays of human emotion allowed me to know I'm richer now than I've ever been. I approached public speaking whether in locker rooms or on stages fearlessly. Imagine the fear of others opinions and the fear to fail. It's very simple for me...I don't chose fear. I have rewritten almost every word in this book. I've done that not out of a place of fear but out of anticipation of winning. Every major project I have made in my story has been fearlessly. There have been times in my story when I have sacrificed so much and resign myself to be Coach Howard. My dreams and imaginations are things within my soul that I chase. There have been moments that have been brought forth that led to the vision for this book. There have been many opportunities and experiences that have shaped me. I can't count the number of people who have worked with me, for me and beside me who collaborated on so many strategies, ideas concepts and projects. I appreciate each and every one of you. Then there's the wise counsel that living life provides to all of us. The moments of solitude which really for me turn into moments with God.

God has been the constant medium in my world.
Starting with birth, my days have been filled with guidance,
support and love. This foundation that God has set for my
life has allowed me to have the faith and the courage to
pursue the call of a lifetime. I am so hopeful that you will
find examples throughout this book that will encourage,
inspire and make you laugh, think and strain to win!

Throughout these words, pages and paragraphs ask
yourself are you willing to step back and observe your
own life? I was willing to step back and look at my entire
life and the story it tells. It has been so fulfilling. In order
to get to this place in my life, I had to go through every
event in this life. These cause and effect relationships
and choices I have made have provide me the willingness
to step on stage, be aggressive in play calling, own and
operate businesses and parent and develop others. Finally,
I was able to step back from my own ego and let God. I
have made some choices that have been tough but for some
reason I always feel like my choices have been for good.
That's Jeremiah 29:11 which I just believe in…it's God's
plan for me. I knew early in my story that life is worth

living and it took a willingness for me to let God work in order to achieve and accomplish.

We shall stand together. Every person who reads this book shall stand together as a winner in the greatest game of them all...the game of life. I'm excited about receiving your stories about the losses, the near misses, the impossibles and watch them turn into wins, overachieves and possibles. Finally, I want to thank every player who has ever played for me. Without you all none of this would be possible. There would be no stories. There would be no adversity. There would be no one to coach and really who is Coach Howard without the players? The football fields, the locker room, the planes, trains, buses and automobiles have all been a great environment for me to share the most special moments that shaped this life. The solemn prayers at the end of games were learning experiences for me to teach and be taught how important it is to care and work together. Seeing progress in others lives is so rewarding to me that I couldn't think of a better work.

By the time you read this, I too would have grown even more. For each time, I speak, coach or mentor; I'm putting an investment in my own future by investing in someone else's. I started this book writing about Dr. Martin Luther King. His most famous speech, the "I Have a Dream" speech has many incredible quotes. My favorite quote from Dr. King is "life's most persistent and urgent question is what are you doing for others?" Once I answered this question...my blessings overflowed, my depression turned to happiness and my story took on a life of its own. I wrote this book based on love. Some love changes, some is dependent and some just varies. The love this dad has for his children never changes but it sure does vary. I've made so many mistakes in my story yet God never has left me. This sort of divine love is the deepest of them all. The Life of My Story is simple...love God love others...be kind and have courage...WIN!!

THE EXTRA POINTS CREED

The Life of My Story
Very simple to me
Began the day I was born
Stopped the day I wrote no more
The Life of My Story
Starts with and stops with all of you
Life is still the truth
Lonely but found
The Life of My Story
Thanks for everything...sharing and caring
There been some sleepless nights
Deep down inside I write
The Life of My Story
Simple to me.
Began the day I was born.
Stopped the day I wrote no more

The Final Point

Most people end their books with two words "The End."
Well if you received as much from this book as I did writing
it...then the two words to end it should be..."The Beginning."
Yes the beginning of a whole new world, a whole new way
of thinking, a whole new will to WIN.

The final point is this. God loves you unconditionally.
Remember that God can father you. I have had so many
adversities and losses and sometimes I just can't understand
it. I'm not perfect but my Father in Heaven I know loves me
and that forces me to respond to the goodness of God.

This is the final point that everyone needs to hear and know.
God wants to be friends with us. We wake up everyday in
awe of HIM. I'm always trying to coach and find the next
great play or player but one day God said "Coach Howard...
Keith..I am extremely fond of you." Brings tears to my
eyes...and reminds me who I am.

I want you to complete this book free of any clutter or
debris...forgive, live life and let go of any baggage. Take a
stand! Pray...rise and be healed and become whole. Don't
fret or cowar (is that a word)...that's the Final Point and until the next chapter...The Extra Point is Up and It is Good!

The Beginning...

CPSIA information can be obtained
at www.ICGtesting.com
Printed in the USA
BVOW03s2245071216

470154BV00004B/7/P